TO LIVE IS CHRIST

THE SISTERS OF MARY
BOOK OF SPIRITUALITY

BY: FR. ALOYSIUS SCHWARTZ

FROM THE PUBLISHERS

In our opinion, Father Schwartz and the Sisters of Mary are the most outstanding Catholic charity in the world. They are transforming impoverished youngsters into future Catholic leaders of the world...and they do it with a smile. Since we have personally inspected this work in Korea, the Philippines and Mexico, we can attest to the outstanding results achieved. The entire staff of Government Institutes is truly honored to serve as publishers of this work by our dear friend Father Schwartz for the wonderful Sisters of Mary. We do this as evidence of our enthusiastic support and commitment to serve the Sisters of Mary whose motto is "Let us serve the Lord with joy" in helping others. Please remember us in your prayers.

Thomas F.P. Sullivan, President
Glory L. Sullivan, Vice President
Government Institutes, Inc.

September 1991

Published by
Government Institutes, Inc.
4 Research Place
Rockville, MD 20850
U.S.A.

ISBN: 0-86587-950-8

Published and bound in the United States of America.

TABLE OF CONTENTS

Dedicated to St. Therese of the Carmel of Lisieux

and to

Sr. Gertrude of the Carmel of Pusan

INTRODUCTION

St. Paul writes, "In word, in action, whatever you do, do all in the name of Christ." To "do all in the name of Christ" means to do all with the mind, the heart, and the spirit of Christ. This is the guiding principle of the spiritual formation of the Sisters of Mary. The novitiate of the Sisters of Mary is modeled after that of Christ. Christ organized a novitiate. His first novices were twelve in number. They were called apostles. His novitiate lasted approximately three years and it produced remarkable results. Upon the completion of their novitiate at Pentecost, the apostles went out and changed the face of the earth.

Christ's novitiate can be described as action-oriented. It was characterized by on-job training, on-site formation, and hands-on learning. Christ, for example, did not take His twelve novices -- the apostles -- to a desert place, a mountaintop, or an enclosed garden far removed from the maddening crowd. On the contrary, Christ and His apostles lived, moved, worked, and breathed in a crowd of people, as a school of fish in a sea of water.

Christ and His apostles were constantly surrounded by a multitude of poor, upon whom Christ took pity and whom He came to serve. At times the people were so numerous that they trampled each other. At other times, the crowd was so rowdy and undisciplined that it prevented Christ from eating, from sleeping, even from praying. On one occasion, this pressing, importuning crowd of people even prevented the Mother of Jesus from approaching her Son. On another occasion, this crowd of people prevented the four friends of the paralytic from bringing the sick man to Jesus.

Christ's program of formation was very pragmatic and highly realistic. Christ intended to train His apostles to serve and to save all men, but especially the poor. The best way to learn is to be among the people whom you are being trained to help and to heal.

One of the very names given Jesus emphasizes this aspect of His *modus operandi*. That name is "Emmanuel" which means "God with us" -- not God apart, separated, or withdrawn, but "God with us," among us, close to us. Jesus looked upon the poor, the lowly, and the suffering, as His friends and He treated them as such. You like to be with your friends. You are at ease when close to them and happiest when surrounded by them. Jesus teaches His apostles by example that they are to look upon the poor, the weak, and the lowly, as friends and to treat them as such.

Even before the apostles completed their three years of formal training, Christ sent them out, two by two, on a practice mission. He sent them to every village in Palestine where He Himself intended to go. This makes eminent sense. You learn best by doing. You learn to run by running, and you learn to swim by swimming. Along these same lines, if you wish to teach someone how to drive a car, you put him behind the wheel of the car and have him practice. This is the method which Christ used in training His apostles and forming His novices.

Christ's novitiate, then, can be described as action-oriented. It can also be characterized as a "working" novitiate as opposed to a "talking" novitiate. The "talking" novitiate emphasizes words, counseling, psychologizing, group encounters, seminars, endless interviews, exchanges, discussions, and so on. There seems to be so much talk, talk, talk, and so many words, words, words, that the novice or the one being trained feels at times as if he or she is veritably drowning in a sea of words.

Christ's style is quite different. Christ shows a repugnance for excessive verbiage. On occasion, He warns His apostles against the pharisees who preach but do not practice, who speak but do not do, who teach but do not act. He calls such as these "hypocrites."

On another occasion in the Gospel, Jesus speaks in a negative manner concerning the pagans who went in for repetitive talk, pious phrases, meaningless jargon when they prayed. "All they do," says Jesus, "is to repeat empty words."

Jesus, Light of the world, loves what is simple, clear and concise. Jesus reflects this outlook when He says, "Let your speech be yes, yes, no, no -- anything in excess of this comes from evil." Jesus had a personality that was attracted to silence and solitude. That is why He went into the desert and spent forty days and forty nights there. That is why He spent nights on the mountaintop. That is why frequently at dawn He went to a secluded place to be alone and to enjoy the silence and solitude. The Prophet Isaiah speaks of this love of silence of Jesus when he writes, "He was lead away as a lamb to the slaughter. He did not open His mouth." This is very much in the spirit of the Old Testament where it is written in the Book of Proverbs, "Where there are many words, there are many sins."

When Jesus did open His lips to speak, His words were always words of life -- that is to say, they were always a call to action. For example, upon concluding the parable of the Good Samaritan, Jesus did not say to His listeners, "Wasn't that a lovely story?" On the contrary, He ends the parable with the admonition, "You, too, go and do in like manner." In a similar fashion, at the Last Supper, after Jesus washes the feet of His disciples, He does not sit down and exclaim, "Wasn't that a touching gesture?" On the contrary, He says, "As you have seen Me do to you, you also do to each other."

Not only does Christ manifest a certain distaste for excessive verbiage and empty jargon, but also, he manifests a certain repugnance for learning for learning's sake, and study for study's sake. To such an extent is this true, that Christ in the Gospel gives a strong impression of having an anti-intellectual bias.

Christ Himself deliberately chose not to attend a formal school of philosophy or theology. Instead, He chose to work with His hands and to be known as Jesus of Nazareth, the son of the carpenter. Again, Jesus did not choose His apostles from the ranks of the learned and the intellectuals, but from among fisherman who, in the Acts of the Apostles, are contemptuously referred to as "ignorant and unlearned."

In the same spirit, Christ on one occasion in the Gospel prays, "Father, Lord of Heaven and earth, I praise You because You have hidden these things from the wise and the prudent and revealed them only to little ones."

In another place in the Gospel, Jesus says, "What man holds in esteem, God mightily despises." Man most esteems learning, study, knowledge, and intellectual recognition. Christ shows a certain holy contempt for this type of person. This is not because learning is bad or study is evil. This certainly is not the case. The intellect is God's greatest gift to man, and man's most precious talent. When properly used, it gives glory to God and service to one's fellow man. But frequently it is misused and so very easily leads to pride, self-exaltation, and self-aggrandizement.

This was the case with Lucifer, the most brilliant of angels, and his companions in heaven. They were blinded by their intellectual brilliance which, in turn, caused them to fall headlong into the pit of pride -- called "hell."

Christ frequently warns His trainees concerning the danger of intellectualism and the seeking of knowledge for the sake of self-aggrandizement. Christ, for example, tells His apostles, not to seek the title of "teacher," nor to seek the title of "counsellor," nor even the title of "father." The father, the counsellor, and the teacher, are superior to the child, the one being counseled, the student. On the contrary, Jesus tells His apostles, "Unless you be converted and become as little children, you cannot enter the kingdom of God." So instead of father, teacher, or counsellor, one should seek to become the child, the student, or the one being counseled.

St. Paul, also, reveals an anti-intellectual bias similar to that of Jesus. Paul was a gifted student who studied at the best school of theology in Jerusalem. The purpose of his studies was the attainment of the knowledge of God. However, his studies produced an opposite effect. They made him ignorant of God and His ways. They blinded him to Christ, who is the Way and the Truth. Through his theological training, Paul was taught that suffering, poverty, humiliation, and death were clear indications of God's displeasure and disfavor. Accordingly, Paul regarded Christ -- poor, suffering, humiliated, and nailed to the cross -- as one who was rejected by God, a false prophet, and a fake messiah. Paul had been convinced by his learning that God could never permit His Son to endure such suffering, humiliation, poverty, and death. Paul's training, then, twisted his thinking and blinded him to the light of the central mystery of redemption -- which is the mystery of the cross.

It was not by his brilliant intellect and superior learning that Paul came to a knowledge of the truth and the light who is Jesus, but rather, by way of grace and self-abasement. On the way to Damascus, Paul was knocked from his horse as by a bolt from the blue. When he got up from the ground, he discovered that he was blind. He put his hand in the hand of one of his companions, and let himself be led humbly as a child into the city of Damascus. For three days, neither eating nor drinking, Paul waited in this state of complete darkness, weakness, and powerlessness. In this state he received the gift of faith and the light of Christ.

This experience was the peak experience in the life of Paul. It shook him to the core of his being and it marked him for life. Thereafter, Paul always had a vague, free-floating suspicion of knowledge, a fear of learning, and a distrust of study. The saying goes, "Once burnt, twice shy." Paul had been badly burnt by his learning which had produced in his soul a sense of moral superiority. Ever afterwards he was very cautious, dubious, and suspicious in this regard. On one occasion, Paul writes, "Knowledge makes one proud. It is charity which makes one perfect." Again, St. Paul writes, "God chooses the weak, the foolish, the powerless, and He puts to shame the wise, the strong, and the powerful. And this is so that not even one man shall glory in the sight of God."

The final goal of Christ's school of formation, as seen in the Gospels, was love. Christ says, "Love is the fulfillment of all the law and all the prophets." Again Jesus says, "I have come to perfect the law and to bring it to completion." Christ teaches that love is the first commandment, and that love is also the second commandment. In summary, love is everything.

St. Paul reflects this thinking of Christ when he writes, "Let charity be the root and foundation of your very existence." St. Paul also writes, "Above everything else, have charity." And again, "Charity is the bond of perfection." In his first Epistle to the Corinthians, Paul also states, "Charity is the most precious and desirable of charisms. It is the most excellent way."

The charity which Christ teaches is basically three-fold -- that is to say it is one, but can be divided into three categories. First of all, charity should be directed towards

God. We must love God with all our mind, heart, will, strength and thought. This is the first and greatest commandment. We practice this first and greatest commandment by prayer. By prayer, in prayer, through prayer, we go directly to God, and without any intermediary, we love Him with all our strength and power.

During the novitiate, then, it is important for the novice to learn to pray, to develop her prayer life, and to perfect this first and foremost form of charity. The novice should strive to pray in a formal way at least three hours a day. Moreover, she should keep a spiritual diary of her prayer life. In her meetings with her directress, she should briefly review her prayer life.

The second form of charity is brotherly love. The novitiate should be a community of love, a loving family -- in imitation of the Most Blessed Trinity. Christ teaches His apostles to love each other when He sends them out on a missionary journey two by two. He indicates that they must first learn to love each other and then, to love the poor. At the Last Supper, Christ stresses the importance of brotherly love. In fact, He calls brotherly love, "My commandment." At the Last Supper, He prays for the grace of brotherly love. He washes the feet of His apostles to teach them in a practical manner the nature of brotherly love. Finally, He institutes the Sacrament of the Eucharist so that they may receive the grace to practice His commandment of brotherly love. Then, at Pentecost, the disciples receive the fullness of the Spirit of Love and they go out boldly, driven by this love; and they share this love with the poor, the needy, the sick, the weak, and the suffering of the world.

The third category of charity can be called love of the poor. This final form of charity is expressed by self-sacrificing service of the poor. Jesus identifies Himself with the poor. To such an extent is this true that St. Vincent de Paul writes, "When we serve the poor, we are serving Jesus Christ Himself."

The novice mistress should adopt St. Therese of Lisieux as exemplar and role model. St. Therese was in effect mistress of novices at the Carmel of Lisieux. As novice mistress, Therese showed herself to be loving, understanding, and compassionate; but at the same time she was very severe, strict, and demanding because this was the way Christ showed Himself to be towards His novices -- His apostles.

In the words of Isaiah the Prophet, "Christ did not cry out in the street, nor did He break the bruised reed, nor extinguish the smoldering wick." Christ was most understanding of the weaknesses of His apostles. He was patient, forgiving, and forebearing. At the same time, however, He demanded total perfection. He frequently pointed out their defects, corrected them constantly, rebuked them sharply, and reprimanded them severely. The mistress of novices -- in imitation of Christ, and following the example of St. Therese of Lisieux -- should practice what can be best described as "tough" love.

The novice mistress must practice not only holy patience, but -- as the occasion demands -- "holy impatience" as well. She should be compassionate but at the same time demanding. She must point out with courage and clarity the defects, faults, and weaknesses of those being directed by her -- especially in this central area of charity. The novice mistress should review with her novices the practice of charity in its three-fold form; namely, prayer, brotherly love, and service of the poor. She should constantly indicate ways of improving, advancing, and making progress in these three categories of charity.

During the novitiate the novices should read, study, and meditate upon the autobiography of St. Therese of Lisieux, entitled the "Story of a Soul." The novices also study the Gospel of St. Luke which has been called the "Gospel of the poor" and which we can call the "Gospel of the Sisters of Mary." Finally, there will be classes based on "To Live is Christ -- the Sisters of Mary book of Spirituality."

In summary, we can describe the novitiate of the Sisters of Mary as a "working novitiate" that is above all, "action-oriented." The ultimate goal of the novitiate is the perfection of charity and the practice of love in its three-fold form.

CHAPTER 1

CHRISTO-CENTRISM

The novitiate is a time of learning. The learning experience is aided, abetted, and enhanced by books. The basic textbook of our novitiate, however, is not one made of paper and ink. It is a living book -- the living Christ.

In the Gospel, Jesus says, "Come to Me, take My yoke upon you, and learn of Me." During the novitiate we respond to this invitation on the part of Christ. We go to Him with faith, sit at His feet, and look into His eyes with love. We open the ears of our hearts, and we learn from Him. We learn especially the secrets of God, Who is love. We learn how to practice love in the triune form as mentioned in the Introduction; namely, prayer, brotherly love, and service of the poor.

The novitiate of the Sisters of Mary is Christo-centric. That is to say, it is not centered on modern psychology, sociology, human words, logic, nor worldy philosophy and reasoning. It is focused and centered on the living Christ, Who is the Beginning and the End, the Alpha and the Omega of the novitiate.

St. Paul's spiritual thrust was also fundamentally Christo-centric. Paul expresses this Christo-centrism in many ways and in many places in his writings. For example, he writes, "It is no longer I who live, but Christ Who lives in me." Again, "The love of Christ has seized my heart." And, "The love of Christ urges me on." Again, in his Epistle to the Ephesians, St. Paul writes, "We must discover with all the saints, the height, the depth, the length, and the breadth of this love of Christ which surpasses all human understanding."

One can conclude from these and many similar phrases in the writings of St. Paul, that Paul had, in a sense, rid himself of all self-consciousness and replaced it with "Christ-consciousness." Paul was more aware of Christ in his life than he was of himself. Christ was more real to him than Paul was to himself. Paul lived for

1

Christ, and Christ alone. Paul reveals this mind-set in many places. For example, Paul refers to himself as "the servant of Christ," "the slave of Christ," "the apostle of Christ," and even on one occasion, as "a fool for Christ."

On one occasion, Christ appeared to St. Catherine of Siena and said, "My daughter, I am all, you are nothing." In effect, this is what St. Paul is saying when he writes, "For me to live is Christ, to die is gain."

It can be said that St. Paul, together with St. Catherine of Siena, and all the saints, were not only filled with "Christ-consciousness," but, in a sense, they were "possessed" by Christ.

In the Gospels, we read accounts of unfortunate souls who were possessed by the devil. Such a person seems to lose his personal freedom and becomes the slave of Satan. The demon which possesses him becomes the source and driving force of all his actions. The devil torments his victim, causes him to go into convulsions, casts him into fire and water, makes him run about, foam at the mouth, and cry out. Indeed, such a creature comes across as a pitiful human specimen.

"Christ-possession" takes on a totally different aspect. This mystical experience is ineffably sweet, gentle, and delightful. Christ Himself refers to the delight of this experience when He says in the Gospel, "My burden is light, and My yoke is sweet."

Moreover, Christ Who is meek and humble of heart never forces entry into the soul of anyone whom He seeks. In the Book of Revelations, Jesus says, "Behold, I stand at the door and knock. Whoever opens to Me, I will enter therein and sup with that person." Jesus, then, stands at the door of my heart as a humble beggar. He knocks softly and gently calls my name with love. Only if I open wide the door of my heart -- by faith and love -- will Jesus enter therein, dwell, and sup with me. In a word, only if I freely surrender myself to Jesus will He seize my consciousness and take possession of my liberty.

In this spiritual surrender to Christ, one experiences the ecstasy of love. The word "ecstasy" comes from the Greek words "ex stasis" which means, literally, "standing outside," "getting out," or "going out." Love releases you from the tyranny of self. It permits you to get out of your self and away from your self. You are lost in Christ-consciousness. You are possessed by Christ, and in this experience is found "the glorious freedom of the children of God" to which St. Paul refers.

In the Gospels, Christ repeatedly speaks of His desire to enter my heart, to dwell therein, and to possess my soul. For example, Christ says, "Abide in Me, and I shall abide in you." Again, "Whoever loses his life for My sake, shall find it." To lose one's life for Christ's sake means to renounce self, to die to self, to get away from self, to be totally indifferent to self, and to seek Christ -- and Christ alone.

Again Christ says, "Unless you hate your own life, you are not worthy of Me." One whom you hate is your enemy. You don't like to think of your enemy, spend time with your enemy, nor be close to your enemy. You wish to hide from him and be as far away as possible from him.

In a sense, "Christ-possession," of which we speak here, can be compared to the hypostatic union. "Hypostatic union" is a theological expression which describes the union of the human and divine nature in the one Person, Christ Jesus. In this simulated "hypostatic union," the soul is immersed in Jesus, and lost in Him. It is possessed by Him to such an extent that there remains only the one Person, Christ Jesus.

People of the world and people without faith simply cannot understand that one can truly love Christ, really fall in love with Jesus, and experience the joy of union with Him -- just as a woman loves a man and is completely captivated by this love. People without faith are convinced that when religious people speak of the love of Christ and their relationship with Jesus, they are speaking pious poetry, spiritual romanticism, or mere religious sentiment without meaning. Nothing could be further from the truth. The love of Christ and the union of Jesus with a soul is something very real. In fact, it is the most real, the most fulfilling, and the most meaningful experience of which a creature composed of flesh and blood is capable of this side of the beatific vision. The union of the soul with Christ is not simply one of flesh and blood -- it is a union of hearts, a oneness of spirits, a melding of souls.

St. Paul with his customary eloquence speaks of the value of Christ's love when he says, "In order to possess the love of Christ, I consider all created things as so much refuse." In a somewhat similar sense, in another place, he writes, "It seems as if I have nothing, but behold, I possess all things."

In the Book of Canticles, the Holy Spirit expresses a similar sentiment with the words, "Whoever discovers love will gladly renounce all that he possesses, and in doing so, consider it nothing."

The goal of the spiritual life is to deepen my personal relationship with Jesus, and to discover Christ's personal love for me. This goal can be best described by simply saying, "I wish to make a friend of Christ." In the Gospel, Christ says to His apostles, "I do not call you servants, but friends." And again, "No greater love has any man than this, that he lay down his life for his friend."

Christ, the Son of God, left heaven, became man, suffered, and died not so much because of His love for the universe, for the world, or mankind; He did this because of His love for one person and one person alone -- namely, me. If I were the only person in the universe, Jesus still would descend from heaven each day and give His flesh and blood as food and drink in the Eucharist to me. It is important to understand this personal, individual, one-on-one love of Jesus for me. He thinks of me, day and night, prays for me constantly, calls me by my name, seeks my heart, knocks at the door of my soul, begs for my faith, and thirsts for my love.

It can be said that Jesus loves me more than my own mother and father, or my closest friend. In fact, He loves me more than I love myself. He seeks my welfare, my good, my pleasure, my glory, my interest, more than I seek these things myself.

St. Teresa of Avila was an attractive woman with a warm and appealing personality. She had many friends and admirers. But she constantly emphasized to her daughters that Jesus was the best and most faithful Friend that one could possibly find. It is written in the Old Testament, "Whoever finds a friend, finds a great treasure." Teresa of Avila found such a treasure in

Jesus, and she lived her life in constant union with this Friend.

In Scripture it is written that "Our God is a jealous God." Jesus, then, is a "jealous" Friend who brooks no compromise.

It is also written in Scripture that "Our God is a consuming fire." Jesus, the "jealous" Friend, enters my heart and consumes in the fire of His love all that is not He. Jesus not only wishes to possess my heart, but He wishes to possess all of my heart.

While a young nun, before she began her own reformed Carmelite order, Teresa of Avila used to entertain many visitors in the parlor of the convent. At that time, this was an accepted practice and in no way violated the rule of the convent. Unwittingly, however, she was compromising her love for Jesus. Thus it happened one day, while Teresa was gaily conversing with her friends in the parlor, that Jesus appeared to her with an angry countenance and rebuked her sharply. He said, "My daughter, henceforth, I want you to converse not with men but with angels." St. Teresa was startled by this apparition and shocked by these words; but from that moment forward, she stopped spending useless time in the parlor. She broke with her friends and developed a greater taste for silence and solitude, which Jesus loves so well, and where one must go and abide, if one wishes to find Jesus, make a friend of Him, and enjoy the sweetness of His love.

St. John of the Cross expresses this ineffable spiritual experience of "Christ-possession" when he writes that, during his entire life, he was always aware of "a certain loving presence within his heart." This "certain loving presence" was none other than that of his Friend, the living Christ.

Edith Stein, a Carmelite nun who died a heroic death in a concentration camp in Germany during the Second World War, writes of her experience of the love of Jesus. She says, "There is a force within me which, while doing no violence to my own free will, has become the source of all my willing and of all my doing." This "force," to which she refers, is none other than the living Jesus.

St. Patrick in words similar to those used by St. Paul, describes his experience of "Christ-possession" by these words, "The love of Christ is within me. It is below me, above me, before me, behind me, beside me -- it surrounds me." In other words, St. Patrick felt that he was totally immersed in the love of Christ. He moved, lived, and breathed in this love as a bird in air or a fish in water.

About two thousand years ago, in a little country in the Middle East called Palestine, the Son of God became man, was born in a stable, and grew up in a town called Nazareth where He lived the life of a poor carpenter for thirty years or so. Then for three years, He lived the life of an itinerant preacher going from village to village, synagogue to synagogue, speaking of the Kingdom of God. Finally, this Man, Jesus of Nazareth, was arrested, crucified, died and was buried. The question now arises, where is this Jesus of Nazareth today? If I wish to find Him, make His acquaintance, make a friend of Him, where should I go? Where must I look? What must I do?

First of all, let us try to answer this question in a negative manner. We know where Jesus is not to be found. He is not in the tomb, because the women and the disciples entered the tomb on Easter morning and confirmed that indeed it was empty. Jesus is no longer in Palestine, because in the presence of five hundred of His disciples, He left Palestine and ascended into the heavens. Nor can Jesus be found in the clouds of the heavens, because we know there is nothing in the clouds but moisture and empty vapor.

Where then is the living Christ today? First of all, the risen, glorified ascended Jesus dwells in heaven -- seated at the right hand of the Father. And He will come again in glory at the end of the world.

But Jesus also continues to dwell among us. He continues to dwell in our world and exert His influence upon it. Jesus continues to keep the promise He made to His disciples in the Gospel, where He said: "I will be with you all days, even unto the end of the world." Jesus continues to be with us and to dwell in the world, primarily in four ways: first and foremost, in the Sacrament of the Eucharist; second, in the inspired word of Scripture; third, in the person of the poor; and fourth, in the person of my neighbor and my brother. The living Christ dwells among us and we can come into intimate personal contact with Him through the Bread, the Book, the Poor, and my Brother.

"Our God is a hidden God," we read in Scripture. Jesus, the Son of God, continues to hide His power and glory in a little piece of bread, in frail human words, in the lowly person of the poor, and in the imperfect, defective character who is my neighbor and my brother.

In the chapters which follow, we will try to examine in some depth and detail this mystery of Jesus Christ: "the same, yesterday, today and forever." We will try to discover this "hidden God" who continues to dwell among us. We will also examine how we can make a friend of Jesus, and establish a personal, loving relationship with Him. In a word, we will try to discover, "with all the saints, the height, the depth, the length, and the breadth of this love of Christ which surpasses all human understanding."

CHAPTER 2

CHRIST IN THE BREAD

Jesus Christ, is alive! He lives among us, and we can come into intimate contact with Him principally through the Sacrament of the Eucharist.

The Eucharist is the main source of grace in our life. Devotion to the Eucharist, then, should be at the heart and center of our spiritual life. From the Eucharist, as from the wounded side of Christ on the cross, flows a never-ending stream of blood and water, life and light, love and faith. We drink from this river of grace when we receive Jesus in communion, when we adore Him in the Eucharist, and when we visit with Him in the tabernacle.

In so many lives of the saints, we read where devotion to the Eucharist was given top-most priority. For example, in her autobiography St. Therese describes her first holy communion as a peak spiritual experience in her life of grace. St. Therese writes, "Before, Therese and Jesus knew and loved each other, but they were still somehow apart. At the moment of communion, there was no longer any apartness -- Therese and Jesus became one. Therese disappeared in the love of Jesus as a drop in an ocean of water."

After her first holy communion, Therese felt in her heart a great attraction for the Eucharist. She constantly hungered for this bread of life. Her greatest joy was to receive Jesus in communion and to adore Him in the tabernacle.

Concomitant with this attraction for the Eucharist, Therese also felt a great attraction to suffering. This attraction to suffering was not just a romantic feeling in the heart of a young girl. On the contrary, it was something very real. Therese asked herself how an attraction so contrary to nature could be felt so strongly. She understood that this real attraction for the cross could be explained only by the real presence of Jesus in her heart through the Eucharist.

St. Margaret Mary Alacoque underwent a mystical experience similar to that of St. Therese of Lisieux. While absorbed in prayer one day, Margaret Mary saw Jesus remove her heart and plunge it into His own. Margaret Mary wrote of this experience, as follows: "It was as if a tiny speck had been plunged into an ocean of fire." Jesus then removed this tiny speck -- the heart of Margaret Mary which was now ablaze with a love similar to that of Jesus, -- then put it back into her own breast. Ever afterwards, Margaret Mary always felt a sharp pain in her left side and could never sleep on that side.

Also, Margaret Mary felt two mystical attractions similar to those which Therese felt. First of all, there was always this strong attraction for the Eucharist and a similarly strong attraction for suffering.

St. Margaret Mary spent hours each day absorbed in adoration of Jesus in the Eucharist. The other sisters in the convent could see her in the evening kneeling in chapel, as close to the tabernacle as possible, completely immobile, her face pale and emaciated, absorbed in adoration of her Eucharistic Lord. Her fellow nuns would come the next morning and see her still kneeling there in chapel, as immobile and unchanged as a statue of marble.

St. Margaret Mary liked to kneel as physically close to the tabernacle as custom at that time would permit. Once, her superiors -- for some strange reason -- forbade her to visit the Blessed Sacrament. Although outside the church building itself, St. Margaret Mary felt herself irresistibly drawn to the Eucharist and leaning against the bricks of the church just behind the tabernacle, she continued to adore her Eucharistic Lord.

In one of his famous dreams, St. John Bosco -- who died on January 31, 1888 -- saw the Church as it exists in our present day and age. The Church was seen as a ship in a stormy sea, blown about by violent winds and battered by mighty waves. The ship looked like it was sinking. Then there arose from this storm-tossed sea two columns. On one column, John Bosco saw the Eucharist, Jesus-Host. On the second column, John Bosco saw Mary, the Mother of Jesus. John Bosco understood that the meaning of this dream was that the Church in our present day and age would undergo violent attack and experience a great crisis. But the Church would be saved by devotion to Jesus in the Eucharist and devotion to Mary, the Mother of Jesus.

In passing, it should be pointed out that these two devotions are closely related. Where Jesus is, there too is Mary. And where Mary is, there too is Jesus.

The flesh and blood of Jesus comes from Mary, His Mother. In communion, when we eat the flesh and drink the blood of Jesus we are at the same time mystically communicating with Mary, His Mother. True devotion to the Eucharist always increases devotion to Mary, the Mother of the Eucharist. Conversely, devotion to Mary will lead to a more intense devotion to the Eucharist.

In 19th century France, there lived a Saint whose mission was to foster devotion to the Eucharist. His name was St. Peter Julian Eymard, founder of the Blessed Sacrament Fathers and Sisters. The mission and vision of these Fathers and Sisters is to adore Jesus in the Eucharist and to propagate devotion to the Blessed Sacrament.

In a sense, our Sisters -- the Sisters of Mary -- could just as easily be called the "Sisters of the Blessed Sacrament" because these two devotions -- to the Eucharist and to Mary -- have priority in our spiritual life and our life of faith.

Mary herself, when she appears to the children of men, always gives priority to devotion to Jesus in the Eucharist. For example, at Fatima, before Mary our Lady of the Rosary appears to the three little children -- Jacinta, Francisco, and Lucia -- she sends an angel to strengthen their faith and love of Jesus in the Eucharist. In April of 1916, a full year before Mary first appeared to the children, an angel appears to the children. The angel -- as the priest at Mass -- is holding a chalice with the host above it. The angel leaves the chalice and host suspended in mid-air, then prostrates on the ground and adores. The angel encourages the children to follow his example, which they do. Then the angel gives communion to the children. Through this event, Mary in effect is saying: First and foremost adore Jesus in the Eucharist, then recite my prayer, the rosary, with faith and fervor.

Another example where Mary gives priority to devotion to the Eucharist can be found in the apparitions at Banneux. Seventy five years after Lourdes, in 1933, Mary appears to a thirteen-year-old child named Mariette Beco. At the time of the apparitions, Mariette Beco was not practicing her religion, and she was not assisting at Mass; in fact, she had not yet made her first holy communion.

During the course of eight apparitions, Mary encourages the child to pray -- especially the rosary. But indirectly, through Mary's intervention, the child begins assisting at Mass again. Also, the child makes her first holy communion. When Mary is asked by the child what she desires, Mary answers: "I want a small chapel." A chapel is a place where the Eucharistic Liturgy is celebrated, and where Jesus-Bread is adored and honored. The point is this, Mary always leads her devotees to more fervent devotion to the Eucharist and increases their attraction for Jesus present in the Bread.

In the Old Testament, God prepares His people in advance for an understanding of the mystery of the Eucharist. Moses, the forerunner of Christ, liberates the Jewish people from the slavery of Egypt. He leads the Jewish people into the desert en route to the promised land of Canaan, flowing with milk and honey. In their journey through the desert, the pilgrim people of God experience hunger and become faint and weary. God sends to them food from heaven, called manna. The Jewish people gather up this bread each day. They eat it, are strengthened by it, and then go forward on their journey. The Eucharist is a new manna sent by God from heaven and given by Christ, the new Moses, to nourish and strengthen the new pilgrim people of God on their journey towards eternal life.

In the Gospels, Jesus also prepares His followers in advance for an understanding of this central mystery of faith, called the Eucharist. On at least two occasions, Jesus multiplied bread and fish, and feeds the people. The words which the Gospel writer uses to describe these miracles are very similar to those used when describing the institution of the Sacrament of the Eucharist. The evangelist writes that Jesus "took bread, blessed it, gave thanks, and then distributed it to the people." The people ate as much as they desired, were filled and satisfied. What is more, much was left over.

These miracles, as most of the other miracles of Jesus, can be considered in a sense as audio-visual aids to His teaching. What Jesus tells us through the multiplication of the loaves and fishes is this: As I give your bodies food, strength, and life, so too will I give your souls nourishment, strength, and spiritual life. I will do this principally by this new manna, this bread of life, called the Eucharist.

Especially in the sixth chapter of the Gospel of St. John, Jesus speaks at length about the gift of the Eucharist, which He will entrust to His Church. Jesus says, "I am the bread of life. Your fathers ate manna in the desert and died. This is the bread which comes down from heaven. If anyone eats of it, he shall not die, he shall live forever. And the bread that I will give is my flesh. This bread gives life to the world."

Jesus continues, "I say to you, unless you eat the flesh of the Son of Man and drink His blood you shall have no life in you. He who eats My flesh and drinks My blood abides in Me and I in him. As I live by the Father, so too, he who eats Me shall live by Me."

In the Gospel of St. John, Jesus uses the words "life" and "love" almost interchangeably. This is because the life of Jesus is a life for others; in a word, it is a life of love. In this sense, Jesus says, "There is no greater love than this, than a man lay down his life for his friends."

It can be said, then, that the Eucharist -- the bread of Life -- is also the Bread of Love. This little piece of bread gives life to the world; at the same time, it is the source of all true love.

This little piece of Bread is the secret of the Sisters of Mary and their apostolate. If one were to remove the Eucharist from our many chapels, our work would quickly lose its vitality, wither up, and die.

St. Paul writes, "The love of Christ is poured into our hearts by the Holy Spirit." Each morning, during the celebration of the Eucharist, there is a new Pentecost. Jesus enters our hearts, and He pours into them His Spirit of love. In the Acts of the Apostles, it is recorded that when the disciples of Jesus were assembled for prayer, the room in which they were gathered shook with the presence and power of the Spirit. In an invisible manner, the holy place in which we are assembled each morning at Mass shakes and trembles in a similar way.

Towards the end of the sixth chapter of St. John, after Jesus first spoke about the mystery of the Eucharist, the reaction of His listeners was one of disbelief. They exclaimed, "Indeed, this is a hard saying and who can accept it?"

Many thought that Jesus was perhaps a bit deranged. If you interpret His words literally, you would conclude that you have to be a cannibal and a vampire to believe in Jesus. One who eats the flesh of his fellow men is called a "cannibal" and one who drinks his blood is frequently referred to as a "vampire." Many of the listeners of Jesus shook their heads in bewilderment and walked away from Him.

Then Jesus turns to the apostles and asks somewhat sadly, "Will not you also go away?" Peter answers with the simplicity of a child, "Lord, to whom shall we go? You have the words of life."

What Peter is saying is this: "Lord, I too do not understand the meaning of your words, but then, who am I and who are You? I am sinful, my mind is weak, my intelligence limited, and my heart is narrow. You are infinite. Your thoughts are different than my thoughts, and your ways are above my ways -- as the heavens are above the earth. So, it matters not whether I understand. I believe. I believe fully, blindly, and unconditionally, because you have spoken these words and you have said that it is thus." It is necessary to have the heart of a child as Peter, in order to believe in the mystery of the Eucharist. Indeed, a little folly is the foundation of faith in this mystery.

We smile condescendingly when we read that in ancient times the Japanese adored a majestic, snow-covered mountain, called Fuji. Also, we laugh in derision when we learn that in Korea, in days gone by, people adored the village oak tree, as if it were a god. Yet what do we do? We do not adore a majestic mountain or a mighty oak tree, but a little piece of bread called the Eucharist.

A saint once exclaimed, "How the devil hates this piece of Bread, how he fears it!" On the contrary, we believe in it, love it, and adore it with the simplicity and fervor of a child -- as did Peter and the other apostles.

If you enter a church the day when no one is there, it appears empty and deserted. But if you could see the same church through the eyes of God, you would be amazed. You would see that it was filled with angels prostrate on the floor, crying out, "Holy, holy, holy!"

In the words of Jesus, "These things are hidden from the wise and prudent and revealed only to little ones." There is the story of a famous scientist who worked in the laboratory of a university in England. The scientist was an agnostic. A Catholic friend once told him of his belief in the Sacrament of the Eucharist. The scientist replied, half jokingly, "Bring me a consecrated host, and let me examine it under the microscope in my laboratory. If I can discover some scientific evidence of a divine presence in this little piece of bread, then, and only then, shall I believe."

If this were ever permitted to the scientist, what would he see under his microscope? He would see nothing except the external appearance of bread. One does not see Jesus present in the Eucharist through the lens of a microscope, but only through the eyes of faith.

On the day before He died, Jesus took bread, blessed it, gave it to His disciples, and said, "Take and eat, this is My body which will be given up for you." In like manner, He took the cup and said, "Take and drink, this is the chalice of my blood which shall be poured out for you."

Before Jesus spoke these words, the bread was simply bread, and the wine, wine. After pronouncing these words, the bread and wine were changed. They became a new reality, a new substance, a new creation -- the Sacrament of the Eucharist.

Jesus did not equivocate when He instituted the Eucharist. The meaning of His words is perfectly clear. Jesus does not say, for example, "When you eat this bread and drink this wine, think of Me. This will be a souvenir of Me." No, Jesus says, "This is My body. This is My blood." And Jesus means exactly what He says. This is something totally new -- it is the body and blood of the living Christ.

It is not really difficult to believe in the mystery of the Eucharist, if you consider who Jesus is. Jesus is the Creator of heaven and earth. In the beginning, He created all things out of nothing simply by the words of His mouth. He says, for example, "Let there be light," and immediately there is light. At the Last Supper, Jesus, the Creator, does not create something out of nothing; rather now He creates the Eucharist out of ordinary bread made from wheat and ordinary wine made from grapes.

In the Sacrament of the Eucharist, we approach Jesus-Bread with the demeanor and outstretched hand of the beggar. We beg Jesus to give us to eat and drink because we are famished and thirsty, weak and weary. Jesus generously grants our request. He gives us His flesh to eat and blood to drink. We are then filled with His abundant life, love, and power.

We leave the alter, depart from the church, and go out into the world. The roles are now reversed. Now it is Jesus who approaches us in the person of the poor and in the person of my neighbor. Jesus looks at us with pleading eyes and outstretched hand. Now it is our turn to give Jesus in our neighbor and Jesus in the poor food to eat and nourishment to drink. The love and life we have received in the Eucharist, we now give to the poor.

"Freely have you received, freely give," says Jesus in the Gospel. The life and grace we gratuitously receive in the Eucharist, we generously share with the poor and our brothers and sisters.

In conclusion, the Eucharist is the principal source of grace in our spiritual life. The more we receive the Eucharist, the more we hunger for it. The more we adore the Eucharist, the greater becomes our attraction for it. Moreover, if our faith in the Eucharist is real and our love for it is pure, we will also experience a greater attraction to the cross and a courageous desire to suffer and sacrifice for Jesus.

CHAPTER 3

CHRIST IN THE BOOK

Jesus Christ continues to live on in the world today, and to exert His influence upon it. As seen in the previous chapter, Jesus does this principally through the Sacrament of the Eucharist. Jesus is not only present in the Bread -- He is the Bread.

Jesus is also present in the inspired word of scripture. He speaks to our hearts through the divinely inspired words of the Bible. Jesus lives in the Book.

In the sixth chapter of St. John's Gospel, Jesus speaks at length about a new manna from heaven which He will give to His followers, and which He calls the Bread of Life. Whoever eats this Bread will not die, he will live forever, he will have life. He will live by Jesus, Who is the source and giver of life. This Bread of Life is, of course, the Sacrament of the Eucharist. We eat this Bread whenever we receive Jesus in Communion, adore Him with faith, and visit with Him in the tabernacle with love.

"Bread of Life" can also be interpreted as referring to the inspired word of Scripture. We eat this Bread whenever we read, listen to, or meditate on the words of the Bible with faith and love.

St. Peter refers to the words of Jesus as words of life. When Jesus concluded His exposition of the Eucharist, Peter says, "Lord, to whom shall we go? You alone have the word of life."

In some churches today, one can see an opened Bible placed on the altar or on a nearby book stand. This serves as an invitation to the man of faith to come and eat the Bread of Life, which is contained not only in the Eucharist hidden in the tabernacle, but also in the word of Scripture contained in the Bible.

In the Psalms, the Holy Spirit describes the inspired word of God variously as "something sweet as honey," "more precious than life," and "more valuable than silver seven times refined." The Prophet Jeremias writes, "Whenever I found the word of God, I devoured it!" The word of God, then, is something inestimably sweet, precious, and valuable.

It is also a word which contains divine strength, power, and energy. In other places in the Old Testament, the Holy Spirit describes the word of God as "a hammer which breaks rock," "a two-edged sword," and "a consuming fire."

In the Gospels, we can read the account of a touching scene which occurs at the beginning of Christ's public ministry. Christ is standing on the outskirts of a town as the sun is going down on the horizon. From every side, the sick, blind, lame, and those possessed by demons come to Jesus. He places His hands on each of them and they are healed -- because, as it is stated in the Gospel account, "power went out from Him."

This same divine power, contained in the word of Scripture, goes out from it, enters our heart, touches our soul, and fills our being with its strength whenever we read this word and meditate upon it with faith and love.

The words of Christ are the words of the God-Man. As such, they are quite different than the words of a mere man. In the Gospel, after hearing the words of Jesus, the people exclaimed, "He speaks differently than our teachers and leaders.... He speaks with authority.... And never before has man spoken like this man."

In the beginning, before the world was, there was only emptiness, nothingness, and darkness. Christ, through whom all things were created, stood in the midst of this nothingness and said, "Let there be light." And there was light. By His word alone, Christ creates. His words have the power to effect what they express and proclaim. By contrast, human words are weak, ineffectual, and powerless. For example, on a rainy day you can look at the sky and say, "I wish the sun would come out." But your words are quite incapable of making the rain stop and the sun shine.

In the Gospels, however, we read where Jesus stood up in the boat in the middle of the lake and commanded the wind and the waves to be still. They meekly obeyed and immediately grew quiet and still. On another occasion, Jesus stood at the entrance to the tomb and cried out in a loud voice, "Lazarus, come forth."

Lazarus immediately was restored to life, and came forth from the tomb.

One day while Jesus was walking along the shore of the lake of Genesareth, He saw Peter and Andrew in their father's boat mending nets. Jesus said to them, "Come, follow Me and I will make you fishers of men." At once they left all, and followed Jesus. One wonders how it is possible for these men who are fathers and husbands with professional commitments, upon hearing the invitation of an itinerant preacher from Nazareth, to immediately leave all and follow after Him.

The answer to this question, of course, is contained in the words of Christ, which are words of life and power. Christ's words, "Come, follow Me," strike the hearts of His listeners as a hammer which breaks rock and pierce their souls as a two-edged sword. At the same time they stir up within His listeners the burning desire to live by these words.

There is no violence, nor force, nor pressure on the part of Jesus when He speaks these words. Peter and Andrew are completely free to close the ears of their hearts to the words of Jesus and to reject His invitation. Yet, with humble, obedient faith, they open the ears of their hearts and let the words enter. These words stir up in them the will to do, and at the same time they impart the power to accomplish what they suggest and demand.

St. Paul expresses this mystery of faith when he states, "It is God who stirs up within us the will to do, and it is God who accomplishes the doing." In another place, St. Paul writes, "The power of Jesus can accomplish in us immeasurably more than we think of or imagine." Through the inspired word of Scripture, God stirs up in our hearts the will to live by these words, and at the same time, He gives the power to accomplish what the words demand of us.

Throughout the history of the Church, we find many examples of the power of Jesus's words in the hearts of those who receive them with childlike trust and obedience. For example, St. Anthony of Egypt heard the words of Christ repeated by a priest in a sermon: "If you wish to be perfect, one thing is lacking. Go sell all that you have, give to the poor, and come follow Me."

St. Anthony let these words penetrate the depths of his heart and enter the core of his being. They stirred up within him the burning will to surrender himself, body and soul, to these words. Shortly, thereafter, St. Anthony sold all his enormous possessions and properties and gave them to the poor. Then he went into the desert to live the life of a poor hermit and he lived this life to the end -- unto death.

Another example of the power of the word of Scripture can be found in the life of St. Augustine. One day in a garden behind his house, Augustine was agonizing over the depraved life which he had been leading. This life of impurity satisfied the desires of the flesh but left only a feeling of guilt, shame, and malaise in his heart. He heard the voice of a child on the other side of the garden wall reciting in a sing-song fashion the Latin words, "Tolle et lege, tolle et lege." "Take up and read, take up and read." St. Augustine picked up the book of Scripture, opened it at random and read these words from St. Paul's Epistle to the Romans: "Now is the time to awake from sleep; the night is far advanced, the dawn at hand. Cast off all revelry, impurity, lust. Put on the Lord Jesus Christ and no longer make any provisions for the desires of the flesh." Those words struck Augustine like a thunderbolt. And in them, he found the will to change his life and the strength to walk the way of purity.

A similar incident occurred in the life of Francis of Assisi. As a young man, he felt a vague, gnawing, free-floating dissatisfaction with the life of pleasure and ease which he had been leading. He left the town and went into the silence and solitude of the countryside where he sought what the Lord desired of him in life. One day while assisting at Mass on the feast of St. Mathias, he heard the celebrant read these words from the Gospel of the day: "Take nothing for your journey -- no money, extra clothing, baggage, or food." These words pierced the heart of Francis like a sharp sword. Francis immediately gave all his money to the priest, took off his comfortable outer clothing, and, clad only in a tunic tied by a piece of rope, began following in the footsteps of

Christ, the "Poor Beggar." Francis walked the way of total renunciation and abject poverty until his death. The will to do this was contained in the words of the Gospel, and the power to accomplish and carry out these words was found in the voice of Christ.

Another example of the power of the word of God can be found in the life of St. Francis Xavier. As a young student in Paris, driven by worldly ambition and pursuing a secular career, Francis met St. Ignatius of Loyola. Ignatius repeated to Francis over and over again the words of Christ, "What does it profit a man if he gain the whole world and suffer the loss of his soul?" These words entered the heart of Francis and consumed all resistance like a blazing fire. Francis -- in company with Ignatius and five others -- left all and followed Christ. Francis followed Christ to the farthest corner of the earth, to the shores of a wind-swept beach on an island off the coast of China, where he died of cold and exhaustion at a relatively early age.

The inspired words of Scripture contain not only infinite power, but, in a sense, infinite meaning as well. St. Paul writes, "How inscrutable are the riches, and the wisdom, and the knowledge of God. Who can understand His ways? Who can comprehend His designs?"

By contrast, the word of man is shallow, narrow, limited, and poor. But the word of God has an infinite quality. In a sense, it has no bottom, nor ceiling. It contains infinite light, infinite wisdom, and the fullness of knowledge. We can read these words of Scripture, hear them, and think of them over and over again, and yet never begin to exhaust their meaning. We constantly discover in them new light, fresh wisdom, and abundant knowledge.

Since the Holy Spirit is the principal author of Scripture, it is important that we read the inspired words under His guidance. To understand the meaning of any book it is necessary to grasp the mind of the author, and to be on the same wave length as the author. Since the Holy Spirit is the author of Scripture, it is necessary to surrender oneself to His action, guidance, and direction, in order to understand its meaning. St.

Paul writes, "The man of faith is moved by the Spirit." And, again, "Wherever the Spirit leads, follow."

In the Gospel, Christ said, "If I leave you, I will send to you the Paraclete. He will reveal to you the meaning of all that I have said to you." Without the assistance of the Holy Spirit, then, we can not truly grasp the meaning of the words of Christ and all the other words of sacred Scripture.

Slow, meditative reading of Scripture, with faith and love, is an excellent form of prayer. St. Benedict encouraged his monks to practice this form of prayer which he refers to as "spiritual reading."

St. Dominic, founder of the Order of Preachers, urged his priests to, "Preach the things upon which you have meditated." His priests meditated especially on the words of Christ contained in the Gospels. Then they went out and preached with power and conviction that which they had meditated on.

St. Dominic himself found great spiritual refreshment in the slow, quiet, meditative reading of the words of Scripture. Exhausted by a day of struggling to convert the Albigensian heretics in the south of France, Dominic would go to the chapel at night, pick up the book of Scripture, and begin reading slowly and quietly. His spirit would be restored, renewed, and refreshed each evening by this simple pious practice.

St. Therese of Lisieux also discovered that the words of Scripture, especially the Gospels, were her greatest source of spiritual refreshment. As a young person, Therese loved to read *The Imitation of Christ,* the writings of St. John of the Cross, and another spiritual book concerning the mysteries of eternity. Toward the end of her life, however, there was only one book in which she found any joy and refreshment. This was the book of the Gospels. She could almost quote the Gospels by heart. She found in them the light and strength needed each day to follow Jesus and to remain faithful to Him until the end.

In the Gospel, Jesus cries out, "Oh Father, Lord of heaven and earth, I praise You because You have hidden these things from the wise and prudent, and revealed them only to little ones, for such is your will." In the spirit of these words, it is important that one receives the words of Christ with a heart which is lowly, humble, and childlike. Otherwise, the power and light in His words will not be released, and will not flow into your own heart and soul. On the contrary, the word of Jesus leads to condemnation and spiritual death for those who receive it with pride and arrogance. The Pharisees, the teachers of the law, and the leaders of the Jews listened to the words of Christ for three years; yet because of their pride they did not open the ears of their hearts to these divine words. They rejected them. And these words, in turn, became for them a source of spiritual death and condemnation.

Judas Iscariot, also, heard the word of Christ for three years but it bore no fruit. "To whom much is given, much will be required." Judas was held responsible for the words of life which he rejected and which, in turn, condemned him.

In a spirit of faith, humility, and childlikeness, one must be guided in the reading of the Scriptures not only by his own reason, but also by the Magisterium of the Church. Christ entrusted the book of Scripture to the authority of His Church. Christ tells Peter that he has the keys. The one with the keys has the authority to open or lock. So, it is the Church that has the power, the authority, and the right to interpret the word of Scripture.

Christ, according to the words of St. John in his Gospel, "Not only knows man, but He knows in detail what is in the heart of man." So it is, Christ knew that if He entrusted the word of Scripture to the individual interpretation of each man, only chaos and confusion would ensue. This is exactly what has happened in the Protestant Churches. In effect, each member is his own church. There are as many churches as members, because each is entitled to interpret Scripture according to his own whim and fancy. The protestants refuse to submit to a higher authority, and they refuse to accept the tradition and Magisterium of the Catholic Church.

It has been said that the devil himself quotes Scripture for his own purposes. In fact, amazingly enough, in the desert on three occasions, the devil quotes

Scripture to Christ Himself, in an effort to tempt Him and to lead Him astray.

Scripture has also been referred to as a "nose of wax." A nose of wax can be made to move in whatever direction you desire simply by holding a burning candle to one side or the other. In other words, you can find in Scripture whatever you seek if you are guided by human reason and proud intellect. It is important to submit to the guidance and teaching of the Church in order to read and understand Scripture as Christ intended it to be read and understood.

It is necessary to point out that Scripture should not be read or studied in a purely intellectual way. In other words, you should not try to break your head to understand the meaning of each and every passage. Read, taste, eat, and enjoy only that which you can understand, that which appeals to you, and that which you can digest. When you eat a fish you put the bones aside and don't try to chew, swallow, and digest them. You would only choke on them and they would cause you discomfort. In a similar way, you take from Scripture what pleases you, what you can easily swallow and digest.

We should develop a firm belief in the word of Scripture and a great love for this word of life. We should love to read it, to hear it spoken, and to meditate upon it. We should find it more exciting, fresh, and stimulating than the morning newspaper or the weekly news magazine.

In the Psalms the Holy Spirit writes, "The just man loves to think upon the word of God day and night, and even at night while lying on his bed he likes to meditate on the law of God." We should find our joy, our consolation, and our strength in the word of God. What is more, whenever we read it with faith and meditate upon it with love, we come into intimate personal contact with the living Christ. His heart speaks to my heart -- and these two hearts become one.

CHAPTER 4

CHRIST IN THE POOR

Jesus Christ is present in the Sacrament of the Eucharist. He is in the little piece of bread. He dwells in our tabernacles. We bow down before this little piece of bread, press our faces to the ground, and cry out with the angels, "Holy, holy, holy."

Jesus Christ is also present in the inspired word of Scripture. He speaks to the ears of our hearts through this holy book, called the Bible. We listen to His words and exclaim, "Truly, You have the words of life."

Jesus Christ is also present in the person of the poor. This too is a mystery of faith and we discover the divine presence not by our reasoning or intelligence, but by humbling, lowering, abasing ourselves and saying, "Lord, I believe; help my unbelief!"

"Our God is a hidden God," we read in Scripture. Our God is a hidden God because He is a humble God. God humbles Himself and chooses to hide His power and glory behind the least, the last, and the lowliest of forms and substances.

The Son of God became flesh and dwelt among us. He took on the appearance of an infant wrapped in rags and lying in a feeding trough for animals in a stable of Bethlehem. The Son of God continues to hide His power and glory behind the appearance of a poor beggar from Nazareth Who walked the roads and byways of Palestine. The same Son of God hid His divinity and omnipotence behind the form of a failed revolutionary and a defeated criminal nailed to a tree on Calvary's hill.

One must have the heart of a fool and the eyes of a child to discover the divine presence behind such lowly and disconcerting forms and substances. We have many examples in Scripture of the self-abasement which is a basic requirement for faith.

The Magi, following the Holy Spirit -- Who appeared to them in the form of a light in the sky, came to the stable of Bethlehem. They went in, knelt down, adored, and offered their gifts to the new born babe -- because they realized they were in the presence of their God.

St. Peter, despite his many faults, had the heart of a child. So it was that God revealed to him the divinity of Christ, and Peter exclaimed. "You are truly the Son of God!"

The centurion on Calvary, although a pagan, looked at the strange Man nailed to the cross. While others continued to mock Him, the centurion cried out, "Truly, was this not the Son of God?"

Already in the Old Testament, God prepares His people for an understanding of the divine indwelling of the poor. For example, when Abraham -- the "father of believers" -- was already an old man he saw three strangers approaching his dwelling. Abraham opened his heart and his home to these three strangers. He received them as VIP's, showed them respect, gave them food, shelter, and hospitality. Later it was revealed to Abraham that one of the three strangers was God Himself, and the other two were angels.

Again in the Old Testament, Tobias is a model of one who served the poor. In a spirit of sacrifice, he gave generously his food, clothing, and possessions to the needy who were all about him. He buried the dead, and showed them respect even at the risk of his own life. Later, Tobias was the victim of a strange accident. Bird droppings fell on his eyes while he was asleep one day, and he woke up blind. He then sent his son on a journey to a distant land. The son was accompanied by a stranger who turned out to be none other than the archangel Raphael. The archangel Raphael guarded Tobias' son on his arduous journey. The son brought back to Tobias money which he desperately needed, and medicine which he put on his eyes to restore his sight. Through these mysterious event, Tobias was made to understand that what he did to the poor, he did to God Himself. And what he gave to the poor, he gave to God. God, in turn, showed mercy, kindness, and benevolence to this, His exemplary servant.

In the Gospels, Christ brings to perfection and develops fully the mystery of the divine indwelling of the poor. Christ speaks of His presence in the poor and His identification with the poor in language remarkably similar to that which He used when He instituted the Sacrament of the Eucharist.

At the Last Supper, Christ took bread and said, "This is My Body," and then he took wine and said, "This is My Blood." After pronouncing these words the bread and wine changed, and became a new reality. This new reality is the Sacrament of the Eucharist.

In the twenty-fifth chapter of St. Matthew, Christ in a similar manner institutes what may be described as the "sacrament of the poor." Christ very solemnly says, "When I was hungry, you gave Me to eat. When I was thirsty, you gave Me to drink. When I was naked, you clothed Me. When I was sick, you nursed Me. When I was homeless, you took Me in. When I was in prison, you visited Me." He goes on to say, "Amen, amen, I say to you, as long as you did it to one of these, the very least of my brothers, you did it to Me."

Christ continues in the same style, "Depart from Me you evil ones, enter the everlasting fire prepared for the devil and his workers! When I was hungry, you did not give Me to eat. When I was thirsty, you did not give Me to drink. When I was naked, you did not clothe Me. When I was sick, you did not minister to Me. When I was homeless, you did not take Me in. When I was in prison, you did not visit Me." Then He concludes with these words, "Amen, I say to you, as long as you did not do it to even one of these, the least of my brothers, you did not do it to Me."

Before pronouncing these words, the poor were simply poor -- people down on their luck, people to be avoided, and even despised. After pronouncing these solemn and sacred words, a change and transformation took place. The poor were now imbued not only with a new dignity, value, and glory, but the poor -- in a sense -- became Christ, Himself. They became living tabernacles in which dwells a divine presence. Christ not only gives the poor priority, He identifies with the poor and becomes one with them.

Henceforth, whatever you do to the poor, you do to Christ. Whatever you give to the poor, you give to Christ. When you speak to the poor, look at them, touch and serve them, you are, in effect entering into direct, intimate contact with the living Christ.

In the Gospel, Christ speaks of faith in the Eucharist as a condition for salvation. He says, "Unless you eat the flesh of the Son of Man and drink his blood, you will not have life in you. He who eats the flesh of the Son of Man and drinks his blood will not taste death, but he will live forever."

Again, in remarkably similar terms, Christ speaks of faith in the "sacrament of the poor." In the twenty-fifth chapter of St. Matthew, He presents this as a precondition for salvation and eternal life. On the last day the Son of Man will separate the good from the wicked, the just from the unjust. His criterium is just one -- active faith and self-sacrificing service of the poor. Christ will turn to those who actively believe in His indwelling of the poor and say to them: "Come blessed of My Father, take possession of the kingdom prepared for you from the beginning of the world." Then, Christ will turn to those who failed to actively believe in the poor and did not serve them, and say to them. "Depart from Me you evil ones. Enter the everlasting fire!"

In a sense, the "sacrament of the poor" can be likened, not only to the Sacrament of the Eucharist, but, also, to the Sacrament of Confession. We are already given a hint of this doctrine in the Old Testament. For example, in the Book of Sirach we read these words of the Holy Spirit, "Just as water extinguishes fire, so too does almsgiving take away sin."

In the Gospels, in many places, Christ speaks in similar manner. For example, on one occasion He turns to the pharisees and says, "If you wish to be clean in your heart, sell your possession and give to the poor." St. Peter expresses this same doctrine in another way, when he writes, "Charity covers a multitude of sins." Just as the Sacrament of Confession purifies the heart, cleanses the soul, and makes us attractive in the sight of God, so too does almsgiving, charity towards the poor, and service of the needy.

St. John of the Cross sums up this teaching, when he says, "On the last day we shall be judged by love." On the last day the poor, neglected, and the needy of the earth will rise up and judge us. They will decide and determine who receives eternal salvation and who receives eternal damnation.

In this sense, St. John Chrysostom writes, "If you see a poor beggar in the street, kneel down and kiss his feet, because he has the power to give you eternal salvation."

St. Vincent de Paul writes, "When you serve the poor, you are serving Jesus Christ." Again, St. Vincent de Paul, in speaking to his Daughters of Charity, says, "If a nun is in the chapel praying and adoring Jesus in the Eucharist, and a poor beggar comes, rings the bell of the convent door, and stands waiting, what should the nun do?" He answers his own question by saying, "She should leave the chapel, go to the beggar, and minister to his needs. In so doing, she is simply leaving Jesus for Jesus."

Throughout the history of the Church, the saints looked at the poor in the light of faith, and they recognized in them the divine presence of Christ.

We are all familiar with the incident which took place in the life of St. Martin of Tours who lived in the fourth century in France. Martin, a young Roman soldier, not yet baptized, was returning on horseback to the city of Tours, one cold, wintry night. He saw a beggar sitting by the side of the road -- cold, shivering, and pleading for help. Martin had nothing to give him, but the heavy officer's cloak on his back. He removed it, cut it in half with his sword, gave half to the beggar, and then, wrapping the other half about his shoulders, returned to his dwelling. That night in a dream, Christ appeared to Martin clothed in the half cloak which he had given the beggar. Christ said, "Martin, my catechumen, has given Me this cloak."

We read of similar instances occurring in the life of Francis of Assisi, and, again in the life of Catherine of Siena. Francis saw a leper approaching him on a country road. Because of his horror of leprosy, Francis was tempted to turn and run. Francis overcame his natural horror, went to the leper, embraced him warmly as a friend, and ministered to his needs. The leper walked away in one direction, and Francis in the other. Francis turned and looked, and -- to his surprise -- the leper had disappeared. He understood that it was not a leper whom he had embraced and assisted, but the living Christ.

Catherine of Siena was returning home one night when she encountered a half naked beggar on a street corner. In a dark alley, she removed her fine outer apparel and gave it to the grateful beggar. Then she went home. That night Christ appeared in a dream, clothed with the apparel which Catherine had thought she was giving to the beggar; but now it was resplendent with many jewels and radiant with brilliant light.

All of these stories -- whether fact or fiction, matters not -- reveal a constant tradition of the Church and the solid faith of the people of God in this mysterious identification of Christ with the poor, and the indwelling of Christ in the most rejected, needy, and underprivileged.

It is more difficult to believe Christ present in the poor, than to believe Christ present in the Bread, or in the Book. Most of the disciples of Christ simply ignore this mystery and pass over it in blissful silence. They can be likened to the priests and levites in the parable of the Good Samaritan who saw Christ beaten, broken, and bleeding by the side of the road, in the person of the man set upon by robbers yet simply passed by and did nothing.

St. James, in his Epistle, speaks in forceful language, of the dynamic, action faith which is required to follow Christ. St. James writes, "What will it profit you my brothers, if a man says that he has faith but does not have works. Can faith alone save him? If a brother or sister be naked, and in want of daily food, and you say to them, go in peace, be warmed and filled, yet you do not give them what is necessary for the body, what good is that? So, too, faith without works is dead."

Let me give an example to illustrate how easy it is to believe Christ's presence in the Eucharist, yet at the same time ignore His presence in the poor. Suppose for the sake of my illustration, someone -- say a satanist -- broke open a tabernacle, stole a ciborium, went to the local dump-site, and threw the consecrated hosts on the garbage heap of the city. A believing Christian secretly witnesses this sacrilegious act. He runs to the chancery office and informs the bishop and his assistants. One can easily imagine what the reaction would be. It would be one of utmost surprise, shock, and scandal. Most likely, one of the priests, or even the bishop himself would rush to the dump-site, gather up one by one the consecrated hosts from the mud, muck, and the garbage; brush them off, put them in a sacred vessel, and then return them to the tabernacle of the church. Probably, public prayers of reparation would be called for. The story of the incident would be written up at great length in the Catholic press. People would read the account with horror, shake their heads and wonder what this world was coming to.

However, the poor of the world live day and night in the muck, the mud, the garbage, and the degradation of dump-sites, garbage heaps, squatter settlements, slum areas, and relocation districts throughout the world. Everyday, believing Christians see them, but they simply shrug their shoulders and pass the other way -- as did the priests and levites in the parable of the Good Samaritan. If the Christians really believed that Christ was present in the person of the poor they would be more disturbed, shocked, and unsettled by these than by the thought of consecrated hosts being scattered among the debris of the dump-sites and garbage heaps.

Speaking from this dynamic, action faith in his heart, St. John Chrysostom writes, "It is not Christ in the tabernacles of our churches Who is hungry, naked, and cold -- but Christ in the poor." There are many instances in the lives of the Saints where holy bishops and priests sold their sacred vestments and vessels in order to feed and clothe Christ in the poor.

Christ present in the Bread of the Eucharist is in no way a threat to us, nor does He offend us in any manner. For example, the Eucharist does not smell, nor does it have a disagreeable taste. The Eucharist never insults us, hurts us, or robs us of our prized possessions. It does not deprive us of our rest, our leisure, and our free time.

What is more, the Eucharist meekly does our bidding and humbly obeys us. If, for example, the priest puts the consecrated host on the right of the altar, it stays there. If he puts it on the left, it remains there. He replaces it in the tabernacle, and it does not move. It is quite different with Christ present in the poor. To paraphrase the words of Isaiah the Prophet, "There is neither beauty nor comeliness in Him. He is a leper, a man struck by God, One who is cursed. One whom you cannot look at with composure. You turn your face away from Him with disgust and revulsion." If you are with the poor and serve them, you quickly discover that they are neither heroes or saints, nor -- in many cases -- even very attractive people. Frequently they smell. They offend us with their words. They go against our will. They rob us of our possessions. They are ungrateful. They devour our time, and take away our leisure.

In the Sacrament of the Eucharist we eat the living Christ. He becomes our food and drink, our flesh and blood. In the "sacrament of the poor," the poor, in a sense, eat us. We become their food and drink. We say to them, as Christ said when instituting the Sacrament of the Eucharist, "Take and eat, this is my body offered up for you. Take and drink, this is my blood which is poured our for you."

In the Sacrament of the Eucharist, we approach Christ as beggars with outstretched hands and pleading eyes. We say, "Lord give me to eat, I am starving and in need. Give me to drink, I am dehydrated and dying for lack of drink." Christ takes pity on us. He gives us His flesh to eat. His blood to drink. We are refreshed, restored, and reinvigorated.

We go out and the roles are now reversed. Christ, in the person of the poor, now approaches us with outstretched hand and pleading eye. He says, "I am hungry, give me to eat. I am thirsty, give me to drink." We, in turn, give Christ in the poor, our flesh to eat, our blood to drink. What, in effect, we are doing, however, is giving Christ His own flesh to eat, His own blood to drink, because this is what we have received in the Eucharist. The point I wish to make here is that these two mysteries are closely connected, intimately related, and they complement and support each other.

True faith in Christ's presence in the Eucharist will strengthen action faith in Christ presence in the poor. Devotion to the Eucharist should inevitably lead to self-sacrificing, service of Christ in the poor.

The same may be said of faith in Christ's presence in the Book. If we read the words of the Holy Spirit in Scripture we will feel impelled to do as Zaccheus, the chief tax collector, when he opened his heart to receive the words of Jesus. He promised then and there to give half of his goods to the poor and to repay anyone whom he might have defrauded four-fold. Jesus rejoiced and said, "Truly, today salvation has come to this house."

But an exaggerated faith in Christ's presence in the poor can distort and twist our life of faith. Without devotion to the Eucharist, and meditation with faith on the inspired word of Scripture, our approach to the poor can very easily become materialistic, hedonistic, and worldly. It is quite easy without faith in the Eucharist and faith in the Bible to make heroes and saints of the poor, and try to remake them into the image of the successful, materialistic, hedonistic, rich farmer, whom in the Gospel story God calls a "fool" -- then to remake them into the image and likeness of Christ. It is so easy to fall into the materialistic mindset of Judas who complained about the largesse of Mary Magdalene to Jesus: "Were it not better if this perfume had been sold and the money given to the poor?"

It is important that we try to develop a faith which is not only active, but also dynamic and living -- but balanced as well. Our life of faith should include active belief in the Eucharist, dynamic belief in the inspired word of Scripture, and energetic belief in Christ present in the person of the poor.

CHAPTER 5

CHRIST IN MY BROTHER

Jesus Christ is present not only in the person of the poor, but also in my brother who is closest to me.

St. Paul expresses this idea when he writes, "We must do good to all men, but especially to those who are of the same household." St. Peter writes in a similar vein, "First and foremost let us practice more fervently love of our brothers."

Christ, Himself, especially at the Last Supper, clearly speaks of this mystery of His presence in my brother. Christ says to His disciples, "I give to you a new commandment, love one another. As I have loved you, so too must you love one another. By this will all men know that you are My disciples, by the love you have for one another. This is My commandment."

Christ refers to brotherly love as His commandment. Then He goes on to say, "If you love me, keep my commandment." And a little further, Christ says, "If you do what I instruct you to do, then you are my friends." Christ instructs and commands us to love each other as He loves His disciples. In effect, Christ tells us, what we do to the brother closest to us, whom we see, we do to Christ, Whom we do not see. What we give to our neighbor next to us, who is visible to our bodily eyes, we give to Christ, Whom we see only through the eyes of faith.

In another place in the Gospel, Jesus says, "The first and the greatest commandment is this, you should love the Lord your God with all your mind, and all your heart, and all your soul. And the second commandment is like it, love your neighbor as yourself."

The second commandment, the commandment of brotherly love, is like the first, the commandment to love God. In effect, there is just one commandment, love. Love of neighbor is simply another expression of love of God. It is the reverse side of the same coin.

St. John in his Epistle expresses the same truth when he writes, "Whoever thinks he loves God whom he does not see, and at the same time hates his brother whom he does see, deceives himself and he is a liar." In another place in the same Epistle, St. John writes, "Whoever loves his brother is in God, and God is in him."

Christ teaches us both by words and example how to practice brotherly love. Especially during the Last Supper, Christ gives us a moving and dramatic lesson in the keeping of His commandment of brotherly love.

First, at the Last Supper, Christ expresses His love for His disciples by praying for them. With great intensity and fervor He prays for His disciples. He cries out, "Father as We are one, make them one. As We love each other, grant that they may love each other. As We are one in each other, grant that they too may be one in each other." The first and finest expression of brotherly love is to pray for our brothers. In so doing, we obtain for them God's help, God's comfort, and God's blessings.

Secondly, Christ expresses the love in His heart by the kind, warm, and tender words which He speaks to His disciples. At the Last Supper, the Heart of Jesus is filled with depression, heaviness, and sadness; yet, He rises above these feelings, forgets Himself, thinks only of His disciples, comforts, encourages, and consoles them as a mother would a child who is sad and troubled. St. Paul writes, "Say only those things which are useful to hear." Christ at the Last Supper says only things which are positive, optimistic, and useful to hear on the part of His disciples. With great sweetness, Jesus says, "My little children, let not your hearts be troubled, and do not be anxious. I will not leave you orphans, alone; but I will come to you." And again, "You will be sad and fearful, but your sadness will be turned into joy -- and your joy no one will take from you." Again He says, "My peace I give to you, my peace I leave with you." We learn from the example of Christ that we must express the love in our hearts by words of love, compassion, and encouragement. We must always speak only "words of life" -- that is to say words that are positive, optimistic, and useful to hear.

Thirdly, during the Last Supper, Christ expresses His love by His deeds and actions. He gets up from the table, takes off His outer garments, prepares water and a towel, kneels at the feet of each disciple, and with His own hands He washes their feet and dries them. He does the work of a servant or a slave. And after sitting down He says, "As you have seen Me do to you, you must do to each other. You must wash each other's feet, you must do the work of a slave to each other." Again, by the example of Jesus we learn that love is expressed by action, by deeds, and by service.

Fourthly and finally, Christ expresses His love by giving. "It is more blessed to give than to receive," says Jesus. At the Last Supper He gives the supreme gift of Himself in the Eucharist. He gives His flesh as food to eat, and His blood as liquid to drink. And on the cross He gives His life for those whom He loves.

Also, Christ shows a special love, friendship, and kindness toward the one among His disciples who betrays Him, who wounds Him the most, and who offends Him the greatest. He washes the feet of Judas. He gives Judas a special morsel of food, as a sign of special respect and affection. In the garden, Judas, this enemy for whom Christ could feel only a natural revulsion and anger comes toward Him. Christ does not insult him, strike him, or abuse him. Instead, He embraces Judas, kisses him, and calls him "friend."

In doing this, Christ teaches that we must love the most the one whom we like the least. We must show charity toward all our brothers, but especially towards those for whom we feel the least natural attraction. We must embrace and kiss the "enemy" among our brothers and the "leper" among our neighbors -- and make a friend of him for Christ.

St. Thomas Aquinas writes, "Love is friendship." Christ treats His disciples as friends. He speaks to them as close, intimate, personal friends. He thinks of them as friends. He treats them as friends. And this is what we must strive to do. For Christ, we must make a friend of our brothers and sisters, our neighbors, and especially of the one for whom we feel a natural antipathy.

St. Paul in several of his letters describes in detail, under the inspiration of the Holy Spirit, the nature of Christ's commandment and the characteristics of the charity which we must practice towards each other. In his Letter to the Corinthians, St. Paul writes, "The charity of Christ is long-suffering. It is kind. It is not puffed up, nor boastful, nor jealous. It is not discourteous. It does not seek its own good. It is not angry. It does not rejoice with evil. It rejoices only with truth. It does not remember evil. It bears all, believes all, and endures all."

In his Epistle to the Colossians, St. Paul uses similar adjectives and similar terms to express this same love, charity, and mercy of Christ. St. Paul writes, "My brothers, put on a heart full of mercy, humble kindness, patience, and meekness, as you put clothes on your body. Bear with each other even if you have a grievance against your brother. Forgive your brother as God forgives you."

Again, in his Letter to the Galatians, St. Paul speaks of the fruits of the Spirit. The first fruit is "love," and this is followed by "peace, joy, patience, temperance, meekness, goodness, and purity."

We see that the same words occur again and again. Where there is this love of Christ, then, there is always kindness, patience, and meekness.

In this sense, St. Thomas Aquinas writes, "The first effect of true love is the liquefaction of the human heart." In other words, the love of Christ does not make our heart hard and cold as stone and ice. It melts it. It makes it soft, warm, and tender as tears or blood. In a similar manner, in the Book of Isaiah, God says, "I will change your hearts of stone into hearts of flesh."

St. Catherine of Siena always speaks of Jesus as the "sweet" Jesus. This one word, better than any other perhaps, portrays the nature of this new love of Christ. It is sweet, kind, warm, tender, gentle, cheerful, positive, encouraging, and optimistic.

It is recorded in the life of St. Catherine of Siena that one day in a vision, she was mystically espoused to Christ Himself. The one officiating at this mystical marriage ceremony was Mary, the Mother of Jesus. In attendance as witnesses were St. Joseph, John the Baptist, and Michael the Archangel. Mary placed a ring on the finger of Catherine's left hand, which served as a symbol of her union with Christ. This ring was visible only to Catherine and to Jesus. However, on occasion Catherine committed little sins against charity, Christ's commandment. For example, she would become impatient with her neighbor, irritated by a brother, or she would offend someone by a sharp word or a frowning face. After doing this, she glanced at her left hand and would notice that the mystical wedding ring had suddenly vanished. After a few days, the ring would reappear. Catherine realized that by offending her neighbors she was offending Jesus Himself. By wounding her brother, or sister, she was wounding the Heart of Jesus.

In reading the life of St. Margaret Mary Alacoque we come across a somewhat similar phenomenon. Jesus appeared to Margaret Mary in her Visitation Convent at Caen, France. He told Margaret Mary that He was grievously disappointed with some of the older nuns in her little community of contemplative Visitation nuns. Some of these older nuns had the habit of judging their fellow sisters, back biting, and gossiping against their fellow sisters. They did this without thinking and without much reflection. But Jesus pointed to this defect with great anger and disappointment. Moreover, Jesus warned that if these nuns continued in these practices against brotherly love and did not repent before dying, they risked going to hell. Margaret Mary was shocked by this revelation. She came to understand how sensitive and delicate is the Heart of Jesus and that He expects much more from His spouses and His friends than from those who do not know Him and love Him intimately. She realized that the least offense against charity and the least imperfection concerning the commandment of Christ offends Him, wounds Him, and hurts Him grievously.

Again Jesus appears to St. Margaret Mary Alacoque and reveals His Sacred Heart which is a symbol of His love. It is burning, on fire with love, and He says, "Behold the Heart which loves men so intensely and, in return, receives so much coldness and indifference."

Again Margaret Mary Alacoque misunderstands these words, and interprets them as referring to sinners outside of the convent who offended Jesus by their great crimes and failings. But Jesus reveals to her that He is most offended by those within the convent, and He is most deeply wounded by sins against charity, and brotherly love -- His commandment.

We see, then, that whatever we do or give to our brother whom we see, we do or give to Jesus whom we do not see. We do not have to go to the gate of our house to look for Jesus present in Lazarus lying there sick, dying, and covered with sores. To find Jesus we simply turn to the brother, or sister who is closest to us, and if we look at our brother and sister with the eyes of the heart and in the light of faith, we will see that he or she is the living Christ.

CHAPTER 6

THE FIVE RELIGIOUS VOWS

What are religious vows?

Religious vows are, in effect, solemn promises made to God to live for Him and Him alone.

Everyday, people in the world make promises. They make promises to their children, to each other, and to their superiors. They promise many things, and they promise in many ways.

The value and importance of a promise is determined by three things: one, to whom the promise is made; two, what is promised; and three, how the promise is made.

A promise made to one in a lower position is of less importance and value. For example, a mother when leaving the house to go to the market, promises her little daughter that she will buy candy and give it to her when she returns. The mother forgets her promise, and disappoints her daughter. But she attaches little importance to it because the promise was made to a mere child -- to someone in an inferior position.

A promise made to a peer is of greater importance and higher value than one made to an inferior. For example, you promise a friend that you will meet her at the movie theater at seven o'clock. But at seven o'clock you have a headache, so you change your mind and decide to remain at home. In so doing, you break your promise, and disappoint your friend who was waiting for you at the movie theatre. But you attach little importance to the broken promise because, after all, it was made only to an equal, a peer.

A promise made to one in a higher position, a supervisor, obviously takes on greater importance and value. For example, I may promise the Cardinal that I will donate five million pesos to build a chapel in the slums for the poor. Because the promise has been made to someone who is above me and occupies a position of authority and superiority, the promise takes on greater weight and importance. Obviously, I cannot regard it lightly.

A religious vow, of course, is made to one who occupies the position of ultimate superiority. It is a promise made to Almighty God, Creator, Redeemer, Lord and Master, Who gives Me life and breath and all good things. Because the promise is made to one who is infinitely above me, this holy promise, called a vow, takes on enormous importance and significance.

The value of a promise itself is not only determined by the one to whom the promise is made, but also by what is promised. A mother promises to buy candy for her daughter. Candy is an insignificant item, and such a promise is obviously light and insignificant. You promise a friend to meet her at a movie theatre. This too is not something of momentous importance, and as such, is not something of great weight or value. The promise, however, to donate money to build a church is obviously much weightier and more important.

By taking the five religious vows, however, one promises everything. One promises to God all that he has and all that he is. This promise, called a vow, made to God and offering all, is of overwhelming importance and significance.

Not only the person to whom the promise is made, or the object of the promise itself, but the manner, style, and form of the promise also determines its value and importance. A mother, smilingly, promises to buy candy for her child. The promise is made in a light and thoughtless manner. This also reduces the value of the promise itself.

In the Gospels, we are familiar with the promise which King Herod made to his step-daughter, Salome. Intoxicated by wine, King Herod foolishly, in front of all the dignitaries and powers that were in Jerusalem of that time, solemnly promises that he will give Salome whatever she asks for -- even if it be half of his kingdom. After consulting with her wicked mother, Salome returns and asks for the head of John the Baptist. The king was taken by surprise and shocked by Salome's request. But Herod felt he was bound to keep his promise because it was made in such a solemn, public, and official manner. He could hardly break it without losing face and making a fool of himself.

Usually, religious vows are made in the presence of the Blessed Sacrament, before a priest or bishop who represents the Church, and before one's religious superiors and fellow sisters. The solemn and sacred manner in which religious vows or promises are made also add to their value and importance.

Here, it is well to note the mind and spirit of Jesus. In the Gospels, Jesus always puts more importance on the state of the heart rather than on external form, style, and manner.

For example, to pray is good; but to pray as did the pharisees -- in order to be seen by others -- is bad. To give alms to a poor beggar is good; but, to give alms as did the pharisees -- simply to show-off -- is bad. To fast is good; but to fast in order to win the praise of men -- is bad. So we see, what is of greater importance is not the act itself, but the intention; not the exterior, but the interior -- the state of the heart.

St. Catherine of Siena, St. Margaret Mary Alacoque, and St. Rose of Lima, all moved by the Holy Spirit, made secret vows of chastity when they were mere children. But they made these vows under the impulse of the Holy Spirit, and they made them with deep faith and intensive love. Such vows are of greater importance, merit, and holiness than vows made in front of the Pope and the entire College of Cardinals in St. Peter's Cathedral in Rome, with all the pomp and circumstance imaginable and all the applause and fanfare that the world can muster, but made without faith, love, and purity of intention.

Man judges by what he sees on the outside. But God judges by what is in the heart. So, it is necessary to bear in mind that faith, love, and purity of intention are of far greater importance than style, manner, and external trappings.

Throughout the history of the Church, holy people made vows and promises to God in many ways. For example, according to tradition, Mary of Nazareth made a private, secret vow of virginity to God in the depths of her heart. St. Teresa of Avila made a vow to her confessor to always choose what is more perfect in order to please God. St. Alphonsus Ligouri made a vow never to waste time. The early Jesuits, assembled with St. Ignatius at Montmarte in Paris, during Mass, made private vows which they offered together to God. Others take religious vows which are authorized and recognized by the local bishop. Still others make vows or promises which are officially recognized and authorized by the Pope. The early Jesuits at first took private vows among themselves; but later these vows were authorized by the Pope and became pontifical vows. Whether it is a personal vow made in secret, a vow made in private to a confessor, a public vow made simply among religious, a vow authorized by a bishop, or a vow officially approved by Rome is of secondary importance. What is of primary importance is the purity of intention, the depth of faith, and the intensity of love with which the vow is made.

In the Gospels, Jesus Himself abhors all pretension, pious posturing, and religious showing-off. The pharisees were great at this. They loved to wear special clothes, tassels, and phylacteries to appear holy, and morally superior, and to impress others. Jesus on the other hand calls a little child, places Him before His disciples, and says, "Whoever becomes as this little child is the greatest in the kingdom of heaven." It is well to note that Jesus does not call one of the pharisees, lawyers, or chief priests clothed in their holy and pious garments, with their superior attitude, and say, "Emulate one of these. Act, dress, and speak pious words such as these and you will be the greatest in the sight of God." Rather, He chooses all that is simple, humble, natural, and lowly. It is in this spirit that the Sisters of Mary make their vows. They try to do it with no posturing, religious play-acting, pretension, or holy showmanship. They do it with great simplicity, naturalness, and childlikeness because they feel that this is most in keeping with the spirit of Jesus.

Some religious groups go in for holy drama and play-acting in connection with the taking of religious vows. They cloth themselves with bridal garments, wear crowns of thorns, cover themselves in red apparel to signify martyrdom, or bury themselves under black sheets to signify their death and burial to what the world stands for. This is part of their tradition and useful for their particular spirituality. However, this has never been part of the tradition or spirituality of the Sisters of Mary.

A Sister of Mary comes before the altar to promise her life to God in a spirit of deep faith and burning charity. She realizes that the promise must spring from the depths of her heart, not from the lips alone -- and she surrenders herself to God in a simple, light-hearted, childlike manner.

The Sisters of Mary take vows of poverty, chastity, obedience, service of the poor, and three hours of daily prayer -- in memory of the five wounds of Jesus.

The vow of poverty is in honor of the wound in the right hand of Jesus. By this very vow we nail to the cross with Jesus all attachment to material possession and worldly goods.

The vow of chastity is in memory of the wound in the left hand of Jesus. By this vow we renounce physical pleasure and nail it to the cross with Jesus.

The vow of obedience is a reminder of the sacred wound in the right foot of Jesus. By this vow we renounce our most precious possession -- our will -- and nail it to the cross.

The vow of service of the poor honors the wound in the left foot of Jesus. By this vow we renounce our time, our energy, our very life -- and nail these to the cross with Jesus.

The vow of prayer can be likened to the wound in the side of Jesus. From this vow -- as from the wound in the side of Jesus -- flows a never ending stream of love and light.

The Sisters of Mary renew their vows each year at the end of the annual retreat. This practice of yearly renewal of vows is nothing original. The Daughters of Charity of St. Vincent de Paul do the same. The reason for this annual renewal of vows is that it helps to keep one's religious commitment fresh, alive and vibrant from year to year. It prevents one from growing stale, weak, lax, lazy, or mediocre. Each year, the sister renews her commitment and in so doing, that commitment remains vibrant, alive, and full of joy.

St. John of the Cross writes, "To receive all, one must renounce all. To enjoy all pleasure, one must renounce all pleasure." In a word, the way of attaining all is the way of nothingness, emptiness, complete surrender and total abandonment and this is the way along which the five religious vows invite, draw, and lead you.

CHAPTER 7

JESUS, THE POOR BEGGAR

By the vow of poverty I promise to be poor as Jesus was poor.

St. Paul writes, "Whoever is in Christ Jesus must walk the way that He walked." If I am in Christ Jesus by faith and love, I must walk the way that He walked. And Jesus, deliberately, walked the way of extreme poverty from Bethlehem to Calvary.

St. Paul writes, "Jesus Christ being rich became poor for our sakes, so that by His poverty we too may be made rich." Jesus Christ renounced the infinite riches of His Father's house. He renounced the power and glory of God, and He came to earth to live among us. He chose to live among us as a poor beggar. If I truly believe in Jesus, I must also believe in His poverty. If I truly love Jesus, I must also love a life of poverty.

Charles de Focauld writes, "My Jesus, I find it difficult to understand how anyone can pretend to love you and at the same time seek a life which is comfortable, rich, and luxurious."

Jesus deliberately chose to be born poor, to live poor, and to die poor. What is more, He comes to us today in the Sacrament of the Eucharist as a poor man. He chooses to hide His power and glory behind the appearance of a little piece of bread which is so totally insignificant and, in a sense, poor.

Jesus was born in a stable at Bethlehem under the sign of extreme poverty. The angels appeared in the sky to the shepherds and said, "Go to Bethlehem. You will find a child wrapped in swaddling clothes and lying in a manger. This will be a sign to you." The shepherds who themselves were poor men would find the newborn savior by the sign of poverty. They would find a child wrapped in rags and lying in a feeding trough for animals.

Frequently, we mistakenly think of the stable at Bethlehem in romantic and sentimental terms. But the fact of the matter is -- a stable is a dwelling place for animals -- not for men. As such, it is dirty, smelly, and crawling with rodents and insects. It is a symbol of poverty, lowliness, and extreme degradation. By deliberately choosing to be born in such a place, Jesus from the very outset dramatically reveals His attitude towards wealth, possessions, and riches.

If Jesus were to return to earth today as Savior, He would choose to be born in a squatter's hovel on Smokey Mountain, Manila. Or if He were to come to Korea He would choose to begin His life in a shack on the dump site at Nan Ji Do, Seoul.

Upon instructions received from an angel in the dead of night, Joseph rises from sleep and hurriedly takes Mary and Jesus and flees into Egypt. Here the Holy Family lives the life of refugees and displaced persons. Such a life is one of daily insecurity, hardship, and poverty. Here, again, from the very outset we see that Jesus deliberately chooses what is lowly rather than lofty; what is insecure rather than secure; what is uncomfortable rather than what is comfortable; what is poor rather than what is rich. This pattern continues throughout the life of Jesus.

After the elapse of some time, Joseph, again following the instructions of the angel, returns with Mary and Jesus to Nazareth. Here Jesus remains until He begins His public life.

When Nathaniel heard that Jesus was from Nazareth, He remarked somewhat contemptuously, "Can anything good come out of Nazareth?" Nazareth was one of the poorest, most insignificant villages in the poorest, most insignificant province of Palestine, namely Galilee. Jesus chose to be known as "Jesus of Nazareth" -- which is indirectly a title of derision, poverty, and lowliness. When one says, "Jesus of Nazareth," one is in effect saying, "Jesus, the poor man." Jesus could have chosen to be known as "Jesus of Jerusalem," "Jesus of Antioch" or "Jesus of Capharnaum," all of which are titles of honor and respect. But He deliberately chose to be known as "Jesus of Nazareth."

He also deliberately chose to be known as Jesus, "son of the carpenter," not the son of the high priest, the governor, the lawyer, the tax collector, or the centurion, but the "son of the carpenter." In Jesus' day and age one who worked with his hands was considered inferior to the scholar who worked with his head. The carpenter's tools which Jesus used at Nazareth are another symbol of the poverty and lowliness which Jesus prefers, loves, and chooses throughout His life.

Jesus began His public life by leaving the world and going into the desert. In the desert there is nothing but sand, wind, silence, solitude, and emptiness. It is a symbol of extreme poverty. Jesus enters this extreme poverty, emptiness, and nothingness and remains there for forty days and forty nights.

In the desert Jesus was tempted three times by the devil. One of these temptations was centered on greed and the desire for material possessions. The devil led Jesus to the peak of a high mountain and showed Him the world and its riches. Then the devil made a strange statement. He said, "All this is in my hands." Strange words, indeed. It seems that the devil exerts a mysterious power over material possessions and uses greed and desire for wealth and riches to ensnare the heart of man. Jesus rejected this temptation. In so doing, Jesus indicates that He had come to establish a church of poverty, simplicity and lowliness as opposed to a church of wealth, riches, and material possessions.

Jesus also reveals His own lifestyle by His words, His preaching, and the instructions He issues to those who wish to come after Him. Jesus abhors all that is false, deceptive, and hypocritical. So it is His words always reflect accurately His life. His teachings and His actions are one. His instructions are always based on what He, Himself, practiced.

Jesus, then, stands in front of the multitude of poor, destitute, and suffering people and says, with power and authority, "Blessed are you poor. Blessed are you who hunger. Blessed are you who weep now." In effect, Jesus is saying, "Blessed are you who are poor as I am poor, you who live a life of discomfort, hardship, and daily difficulty -- as I Myself do." If Jesus, Himself, did not share the poverty of the people He was addressing, His enemies would have seized upon His words and used them to mock Him.

Jesus on one occasion said to His disciples, "As the Father has sent Me, so too, do I send you." Jesus sent His disciples and apostles on missionary journeys. He gives them clear instructions about how they are to live and conduct themselves. In effect, He tells them to live as He Himself was living, and to conduct themselves as He conducted Himself.

Jesus instructed them, "Take no money, no extra clothing, no food for the journey." And He goes on to add, "Do not go from one house to another. Whatever house you enter, remain there and eat what is given you." He doesn't want His disciples to wander from one house to another, seeking better living conditions and more delicious food. They are to be totally indifferent to material possessions. In the words of St. Francis de Sales, "Refuse nothing, ask for nothing." They are to be totally abandoned to God's providence. They are instructed to practice holy indifference and absolute poverty, as did Jesus Himself.

On another occasion, Jesus said to someone who wanted to come after Him, "The foxes have dens; the birds of the air have nests; but the Son of Man has nowhere to lay His head." Someone who has nowhere to lay his head is a vagrant, a homeless person, a beggar. Jesus Himself lived this life for three years, completely dependent on the charity of others for his livelihood and daily sustenance. Because of this, St. Dominic refers to Jesus as, "the naked beggar;" and St. Francis of Assisi speaks of Jesus as, "the poor beggar."

On another occasion, in the Gospel, Jesus tells the rich, young man, whom He loved, "If you wish to be perfect, one thing is lacking to you. Sell all that you have, give to the poor, and come follow me." Because Jesus Himself had done this very thing -- namely, He had renounced all the possessions of His Father's house, sacrificed everything, and had become totally poor -- He could ask the same sacrifice of His disciples, followers, and friends. The rich, young man hesitated and then walked away because he had many possessions.

Although Jesus loved him, He did not call him back and work out a compromise. Jesus could have said, for example, "If this is a little too much for you, begin by selling fifty percent of what you possess and keep the rest as security for the future. It might be a little too much for you to burn your bridges from the very beginning, because, after all, you do not know what is going to happen to Me, and there is no insurance for when you become sick or old."

There is an almost fanatical streak in Jesus and He brooks no compromise. He invites His followers not only to poverty but to extreme, absolute poverty and unconditional renunciation. In the Gospel it is written, "Many are called, but few are chosen." Jesus calls many to this total renunciation and absolute poverty, but He has few takers. Few there are who are willing to respond. That's the way it was then, and that's the way it is now.

Jesus, in another place in the Gospel, says, "Unless you renounce all that you possess, you cannot be My disciple." Each of His disciples and apostles upon hearing the call of Jesus, left all immediately without hesitation, and followed Jesus. Such sacrifice, risk, and daring are beyond the power of men. But the word of Jesus is the "word of life." If one receives this word of life with faith, it stirs up within the will to do and the power to accomplish it.

Jesus, by deliberate choice, was born poor, lived poor, and finally He died poor. Jesus nailed to the cross on Calvary is a symbol of extreme poverty. He is stripped of His clothing, and stripped of His reputation. He gives His strength, His blood, and finally His life. Then a soldier comes and pierces His side, and there flows out blood and water. He totally empties Himself, gives all that He has to give, and dies in absolute nothingness and poverty.

Jesus gives a dramatic, compelling example of poverty throughout His life. Moreover, He asks His disciples to choose this same ideal and to constantly strive to realize it in their daily lives.

In this sense, St. John of the Cross writes, "If you wish to imitate Jesus Christ, you must always choose what is poor rather than what is rich, what is uncomfortable rather than comfortable, what gives pain rather than pleasure, what is lowly rather than what is exalted, what is less rather than more, what causes worry rather than what gives rest and ease, what gives work rather than what gives tranquility." And again, John of the Cross writes, "If you wish to possess all, you must renounce all."

In the writings of St. John of the Cross one frequently comes upon the word "nada, "which means "nothingness," "emptiness"and "total poverty." "Nada," he writes, "is the name of the road which leads us to the peak of Mount Carmel -- the mount of perfection and holiness."

The first Christians, who understood in a fresh, vibrant way the mind and spirit of Christ, practiced a form of poverty. They sold their possessions, gave them to the apostles, and lived a life of holy communism.

In the Acts of the Apostles we read where Peter and John were going to the temple one afternoon to pray. A crippled beggar looks up at them pleadingly, hoping and expecting alms. Peter stops and says, "Silver and gold I have none, but what I have I give to you. Take up your pallet and walk." And the crippled beggar got up and began to walk, and run, and to give praise and glory to God. Peter and John, as did the other apostles, had no gold nor silver. They were poor men and beggars as was Jesus, their master. But in this poverty of Jesus is found the power to perform miracles and the grace to heal, to help, and to serve. Freedom from material possessions, and renunciation of wealth gives one a certain divine power, force, and energy for good.

In the life of St. Dominic we read that one day during a visit to Rome, the Pope gave him a guided tour of the Eternal City. With pride the Pope pointed out the impressive churches, imposing structures, and wealthy buildings which belonged to the Church. Jokingly, the Pope remarked, "The Church today can no longer say, as did Peter in the Acts of the Apostles, gold and silver I have none." St. Dominic simply replied, "You Holiness, by the same token, the Church can no longer say -- as did St. Peter in the Acts -- take up your pallet and walk." The meaning of St. Dominic's remark is clear and poignant. A Church of poverty, lowliness, and renunciation is a Church of miracles -- a Church from which the power of Jesus will continue to flow, operate, and to work good.

St. Paul, who had the same mind and spirit of Jesus, also deliberately chose a life of daily poverty, simplicity, and renunciation. He made it a point of honor never to accept money from his Christians. Instead, he chose to earn his daily bread by working as a tent-maker with his own hands. On one occasion St. Paul wrote enigmatically, "Although it seems as if I have nothing, in effect, I possess all." What Paul means is, although he has no material possessions, or money, and seems very destitute, in fact he possesses the power and presence of Christ in his heart.

St. Francis of Assisi has been described by one pope as, "the most perfect model of Jesus Christ who ever lived." St. Francis was also a perfect model of poverty. His special calling was to give dramatic witness to the poverty of Jesus, and this he did with great gusto, originality, and playfulness. As most saints, and as Jesus Himself, Francis too carried things to the extreme. For example, St. Francis refused to own even a book. He referred to poverty as his bride, and he chose her as his constant companion. He had such a love of the poverty of Jesus that when he was dying his final request was to be stripped of his outer clothing and laid on the bare ground, as the naked Jesus on the cross. As Jesus, Francis too lived poor and died poor; and gave remarkable witness to Jesus, the "Poor Beggar."

How does the Sister of Mary imitate the poor Jesus? How does she practice the vow of poverty in her daily life?

First of all, she aspires to a life of utmost simplicity. She realizes her body is an instrument of service and as such it does not belong to her; it belongs to Jesus in the poor. So she must take good care of her body. Also, she keeps in mind the admonition of St. Paul, "Above all else have charity." So she interprets the vow of poverty always in the light of charity -- which is the queen of virtues. With these parameters in mind, however, she can live a life of real simplicity, renunciation, and practical poverty.

Real poverty hurts. It causes pain and requires sacrifice. St. Francis de Sales writes, "Many would like to have the reputation of being poor, and at the same time live comfortably and pleasantly." This is mere pious play acting, and is far removed from the practical poverty which Jesus holds as an ideal to his disciples.

First of all, the Sister of Mary practices poverty in the area of eating. She prefers food which is good and nourishing, but simple. Also, she mortifies her appetite and always practices temperance. It is somewhat unseemly for one who pretends to live poor and who speaks of renouncing all things, yet at the same time has an obsessive interest in food, is very attached to the pleasure of eating, and in fact, habitually overeats. It is a bit hypocritical to speak of following Jesus, the poor beggar, when one is excessively overweight, simply because he cannot control his appetite and habitually eats too much.

The Sister of Mary practices poverty with regard to her health. She takes reasonable care of her health, but she takes care not to become a holy hypochondriac as so many religious are inclined to become. The religious, especially the contemplative, tend to become introverted and overly preoccupied with self and one's health; and thus, every little ache, pain, and discomfort takes on an exaggerated importance. Too many religious try one form of medication after another, go to one doctor after another, and seek this cure and that cure.

In the Gospel of St. Mark, it is interesting to read that the woman who had an issue of blood for twelve years went from one doctor to another. She used up all her money, and her condition only got worse. Frequently this is the way it is with medical care. It has been estimated that eighty percent of those who see doctors have ailments that are psychosomatic in origin. They complain most frequently of headaches, backaches, indigestion, and colds. The best cure for these types of ailments is frequently to forget about them. It has also been estimated that about eighty percent of internal, medical problems heal in a natural manner without any care or medication and simply go away on their own. Also, it has been estimated that only about one out of five of those who are hospitalized for internal medical reasons benefit in any way by their stay. St. Teresa of Avila remarked that her fragile health became better the less she thought about it and the less she was concerned with it.

The Sister of Mary also practices a form of poverty by renouncing security for the future. Perhaps one of the reasons the rich young man in the Gospel story hesitated to follow Jesus was because Jesus could not offer him total security for the future. Jesus, Himself, says, "Do not be concerned about tomorrow." Too many religious seem overly concerned with social security, insurance plans, and absolute assurance that all will be well provided for them, today, tomorrow, and forever. The Sister of Mary, in the spirit of Christ, strives to live from day to day, hour to hour, instant to instant, completely abandoned to God's providence, totally dependent on His mercy, and trusting blindly in His love.

The Sister of Mary practices poverty in the area of education. She does her best to develop all her talents and ability in order to better serve the poor. But at the same time she is in no way interested in diplomas, degrees, and intellectual pursuits for their own sake. It is so easy to pursue the path of intellectual advancement for one's own self-aggrandizement under the pretext of doing good and better serving the poor. The intellect, of course, is God's most precious gift to man and as such we must develop it fully. However, there is always an inherent danger to pride in intellectualism and the exaggerated pursuit of knowledge, learning, and higher education. Like Jesus, her model and mentor, the Sister of Mary seeks always what is poor, humble, and lowly. Also it is a fact that one acquires a greater knowledge of the poor and learns to serve them effectively by the practice and experience of everyday poverty, rather than by the pursuit of intellectualism, diplomas, and degrees.

The Sister of Mary practices poverty by freely giving her time, her freedom, and her leisure. As Jesus, she lets herself be devoured and consumed by the poor whom she serves. It is so easy for a religious to become attached to leisure, free time, and the lack of responsibility. But the Sister of Mary renounces leisure, and gives herself, body and soul, to Jesus in the poor.

The Sister of Mary also practices poverty by renouncing worldly glory, praise, recognition, and approbation. She seeks only the approval of God. It is interesting to note that the Gospel model of one who serves the poor is the Good Samaritan rather than the priest, or the deacon who enjoyed the approval of the then existing church authorities. The Good Samaritan was considered and treated as a heretic in his day and age, and was held in contempt by those in ecclesiastical authority. Mary Magdalene, also, whom Jesus holds up as a model of the contemplative and whom He makes His most intimate friend was considered and treated as a sinner and an outcast by those who held positions of authority in the church. Jesus, Himself, did not enjoy the acceptance or approval by the authorities of His day. After Jesus cast the money changers out of the temple, the leaders of the Jews asked contemptuously, "By what authority do you do these things?"

A chapter devoted to the vow of poverty would not be complete without some reflection on the spirit of poverty.

In the Gospel of St. Luke, Jesus says, "Blessed are you poor." Jesus, here, refers to material, economic, everyday poverty.

But in the Gospel of St. Matthew Jesus says, "Blessed are the poor in spirit." Here He refers to poverty of heart, which is a total detachment from all that is not God. Poverty of spirit can be described as passive poverty, a total, joyful acceptance of that poverty which God chooses for one.

An example of this poverty of spirit can be found in the story of Job. God deliberately takes from Job all that he cherishes, all that gives him pleasure and delight, all that he is attached to. God takes from him his possessions, his flocks, his wealth, his riches, his children, and finally his health and his reputation, and even his friends. Job stands on a dung hill as a symbol of poverty -- very much like Jesus on the Cross. Job accepts this poverty which is sent by God with joy and gratitude, with calm and serenity. Active poverty and material poverty can be considered as a preparation for this higher form of poverty which can be described as passive poverty -- that poverty which God chooses and sends to us.

Passive poverty implies holy indifference, complete abandonment, total surrender, and joyful acceptance of all that Gods sends to one. If God touches one's flesh and robs him of strength, comfort, ease, health, and even life itself he can accept this with peace, joy, and gratitude. If God robs one of his reputation he accepts this also. If God robs one of his friends or whomever or whatever he is attached to, he accepts all this with calm, serenity, and holy indifference.

The vow of poverty, then, means to be poor as Jesus, actively and passively poor, materially and spiritually poor. In this poverty of Jesus is found the riches of God, the fullness of grace, and the power to perform miracles.

CHAPTER 8

JESUS, FAITHFUL FRIEND

St. Paul writes, "We must be pure as Jesus is pure."

By the vow of chastity I promise to be pure as Jesus is pure and to embrace a life of chastity as did Jesus.

In order to give us an example, Jesus deliberately chose to live a life of celibacy and uncompromising chastity. Moreover, He chooses His mother from among the ranks of spotless virgins. His foster father, Joseph, was also a celibate. The disciple John, whom He loved, the one who leaned on His breast at the Last Supper with such familiarity, was also a virgin. And St. Paul who is the mirror image of Christ, after his conversion, lived a life of virginity and total chastity.

In the Gospel, Jesus extols the value of virginity and the desirability of chastity. He says, "There are celibates and virgins who make this sacrifice in order to possess the kingdom of God." The "kingdom of God" is another way of saying the fullness of holiness, peace and joy in the Spirit.

Again Jesus in the Gospel says, "Blessed are the pure of heart, for they shall see God." Jesus could speak these words boldly and forcefully because He Himself was an example of purity and lived a life of spotless chastity.

For three years Jesus was surrounded by His enemies, as a lamb by wolves. They constantly snapped, snarled, bit, and tore at Him. They were constantly looking for faults, weaknesses, and mistakes with which to reproach Him, accuse Him, and attack Him.

They accused Jesus of being a glutton and a wine drinker. They said He was possessed by a demon, and was the prince of devils. They called Him a blasphemer, a false prophet, an insurrectionist, and a troublemaker. They accused Him of many things, but never of any impropriety in the area of chastity. The reason for this is that His life was totally beyond reproach in this area.

A life of virginity is a life of constant sacrifice. It is not a game, child's play, nor a laughing matter to embrace a life of permanent virginity. It means to deny satisfaction of one of the strongest impulses in a creature made of flesh and blood. It requires constant vigilance, self control, and dying to self. A life of perfect chastity has been aptly compared to a life of daily martyrdom.

In the early Church, fervent followers of Christ expressed their burning love for Him by shedding their blood, and by freely accepting martyrdom. After a while there was no longer the opportunity for martyrdom, because the Church was now accepted and Christians were given their proper place in society. Now those who aspired to a more intense love of Christ chose the path of virginity. This quiet sacrifice of virginity now replaces the dramatic sacrifice of martyrdom. It is a form of "white" martyrdom. There is no dramatic shedding of blood nor instant death, but only a quiet, daily, dying to self. In many ways, however, this "white" martyrdom of virginity requires the same courage and renunciation as "red" martyrdom.

However, it is important to stress the positive aspects of chastity rather than to dwell on its negative features. Chastity should not be viewed so much as the renunciation of physical pleasure and the natural joy of marriage and family, but rather as the choosing of Christ as friend, spouse, and bridegroom.

A life of chastity is a life of union with Christ. It is difficult for people of the world to truly believe that a soul can establish a relationship with Christ which is much more intimate, satisfying, and real than the relationship between a husband and a wife.

The Book of Canticles compares this union of the soul with God to the love of a shepherd girl for a shepherd boy. This beautiful love story concludes with the words, "Whoever finds this love, will renounce all things and consider them as nothing." St. Paul expresses this in similar words, when he writes, "In order to possess the love of Christ I regard all created things as so much refuse and loss."

It is because of the joy, peace, and spiritual pleasure which is found in chastity that Jesus declares the pure of heart to be blessed. In a life of chastity there is a new, secret, spiritual pleasure which comes from God. On occasion in the Gospel, this pleasure is called "peace," "joy," and "glory." It is something very real, sweet, and delightful. It begins in this life and reaches its fullness in the next.

In the Gospel, someone approaches Jesus with a theological riddle. A woman had seven husbands. Each died, one after another. In the next world who would possess this woman as his wife? Jesus answered, "In the next life there is no eating or drinking, marrying, or giving in marriage, but men will be as angels." In effect, Jesus is saying in the next life we will enjoy a new pleasure which is a spiritual pleasure -- the pleasure of the angels. In this sense, it is written in Scripture, "You will be as gods." This new pleasure -- secret, spiritual, and springing from the depths of the heart -- is the reward for a life of chastity.

"Our God is a jealous God," we read in Scripture. Jesus, then, is a jealous friend, spouse, and lover. So it is, that it is not enough to aspire to a life of chastity, but one must aspire to a life of total, perfect, and uncompromising chastity. One must be chaste and permanently chaste, totally and perfectly chaste in mind and heart, word, look, and action.

Such sublime chastity is beyond the power of man. "Unless the Lord gives it, there is nothing which man can receive," says John the Baptist in the Gospel. Chastity is a grace. Of myself and by myself I can be chaste for a certain period of time, but not permanently. Of myself and by myself I can be partially chaste, but not completely and totally chaste. I realize my own weakness and powerlessness in this area and humbly and constantly beg for the grace of perfect and total chastity.

So far this reflection on chastity has been somewhat speculative. Now let us consider chastity from a more practical point of view. How do I practice chastity and guard, preserve, and strengthen it in my everyday life?

First of all, it is essential that one practices habitual mortification in order to live a life of Christ-like chastity. St. Charles Borromeo wrote, "It is almost impossible for a young person who does not practice some form of mortification to live a life of true chastity."

St. Paul in his Letter to the Colossians writes, "My brothers you must practice mortification in your bodily members." Again, St. Paul speaks to the Corinthians, "I chastise my body and bring it into subjection." And, again, in another one of his Epistles, he writes, "My brothers do not seek to satisfy the desires of the flesh." In a similar vein, St. Paul writes, "We must mortify our bodies and nail its lust and desires to the cross of Christ."

Mortification should be focused on three areas. First, mortification in the area of eating -- with regard to both quality and quantity of food. There should always be restraint of this compulsive desire to eat more and more, and to constantly seek the satisfaction of this bodily appetite. If one cannot control the appetite for food it is well nigh impossible to control the appetite for sexual pleasure which is much stronger.

Second, one must practice mortification of the eyes. One cannot simply look at what one wishes to look at, and read what one wishes to read, and constantly satisfy one's curiosity. There must be constant custody of the eyes and mortification of curiosity. In this regards, St. Augustine writes, "It is possible to commit mortal sin with one's eyes, not simply by reading something impure, but by the way one looks at another person." One must get in the habit of "looking, without seeing" -- and not turning back for a second look at someone or something which catches one's fancy. This requires constant vigilance and self-control, especially in our modern world.

Third, one must mortify oneself interiorly in the area of thought. Action follows thought. If one constantly thinks impure thoughts, he will inevitably commit impure acts. One must constantly guard the entry to his heart and refuse admittance to any thought, memory, or imagination which is not in accordance with the chastity of Christ. This is not easy and it requires constant inner struggle, alertness, and effort.

Theologians write concerning the "sin of surprise." However, it is rare indeed for one to commit a serious sin against chastity by surprise. Such a sin is usually subtly prepared by habitual neglect of mortification in the area of eating, seeing, and thinking.

Just as mortification prepares the heart for a life of chastity, so too does modesty protect and preserve it.

Chastity can be compared to a flower garden which is lovely, fragrant, and attractive. But the garden must be protected from animals or people who would trample on the flowers by a hedge which is high, strong, and solid. The hedge which protects the flower garden of chastity is called "modesty."

Modesty can be defined as holy shyness, holy reserve, a holy sense of decorum, or a holy sense of shame. Modesty is that invisible line of which one is always aware and which one never crosses under any circumstances. A person who is modest always practices propriety in dress, speech, demeanor, look, and action. On the contrary, a person who is immodest is bold, brazen, and lacking in reserve, shyness, or sense of shame -- especially with regard to the opposite sex.

Mary of Nazareth shows this holy reserve and shyness at the moment of the Visitation. An angel in the form of a radiant young man appears suddenly one day while she is alone in her room. Mary is immediately frightened. She is on her guard and ready to flee. This is the reaction of a heart which is modest, and a person who is pure and chaste.

The virtue of modesty is seen in the lives of all the saints. For example, St. Francis de Sales had the reputation of being a saint. This "living saint" was staying overnight in the house of a wealthy friend. The friend in question had a carpenter secretly bore a hole in the bedroom where Francis was staying. At night the friend watched Francis while he was alone to see how he conducted himself. The friend watched him at night and even during the day, and was greatly impressed by the holy modesty, reserve, and propriety of St. Francis even when he thought he was alone and no one was watching him but the saints and angels.

If modesty is the hedge which protects the virtue of chastity, then humility can be spoken of as the watchdog which guards it. A person who is humble always has a holy suspicion, doubt, and distrust of self. He is never over-confident, complacent, nor self-satisfied. St. Peter, in the Gospel, lacked this humility and trusted in himself too much. He declared, "Lord, I will never deny you, I will even offer my life for you." "Pride goeth before the fall." The pride of Peter caused him to stumble, to fall, and to deny his Lord on three occasions.

St. Philip Neri used to pray, "Lord, beware of Philip, he can betray you." As seen in this prayer, the saints always possess a holy, humble, and realistic understanding of their weakness and a certain healthy, and holy distrust of self. In this sense St. Paul writes, "Whoever thinks he stands, must beware lest he fall."

One who is humble of heart lives his life in the light of Jesus. His heart is an open book before Jesus, before his confessor, and before his spiritual director. One who is humble has the courage to overcome his pride, shame, and sense of personal honor. He brings into the light all temptations, doubts, problems, mistakes, and failures in this area of chastity. Whenever there is any problem whatsoever he does not try to hide it out of a sense of false shame. With simplicity and childlikeness, he expresses it in confession, or when he receives spiritual direction.

St. John Vianney is "the saint of the confessional." At times he would spend as many as fourteen hours a day hearing confessions. He was a virtuoso of the confessional. He once remarked that the devil is most active outside of the confessional. The devil is the spirit of darkness, so he hates the Sacrament of Confession, which is a sacrament of light. The devil, according to the experience of St. John Vianney, tries to confuse penitents, and out of a false sense of shame he tries to prevail upon them to make bad confessions -- especially concerning sins against purity. However, if the penitent is determined and resolved to confess such sins, then the devil tries to persuade him to confess these sins in a very vague, incomplete, and partial manner.

We should be aware of this strategy of the devil and constantly approach confession and spiritual direction as a child of light and an open book. If we develop this habit early in our religious life -- no matter what difficulty or temptation assails us -- we will always be able to find peace, and to preserve inner serenity and innocence.

To preserve the virtue of chastity one must also avoid, not only sin, but the occasion of sin as well. "Whoever loves danger will perish therein," writes St. Paul. Because St. Peter approached the occasion of sin and drew close to temptation he fell and erred. The alcoholic commits a sin of drunkenness the moment he enters a beer hall. By past experience he knows that by placing himself in the proximity of sin he will inevitably fall and fail.

Whenever we recite the Our Father we conclude with the words, "Lead us not into temptation." By these words we ask God to show us in His light all the possible occasions of sin, proximate and remote; and we ask Him to give us the good judgment, prudence, and strength of character to avoid them. No matter how strong a person thinks he is, if he is placed in certain circumstances he will be weakened, lust can seize him as a demon, and throw him into the fire of sexual sin.

The devil is a fallen angel whose name is Lucifer, which means the "bearer of light." He is a brilliant strategist, and so it is especially in the area of chastity that he tries to tempt us and trap us up under the "pretext of good." The devil will try to deceive us and make us reach for the forbidden fruit under the pretense of virtue. For example, one reads an impure book in order to acquire knowledge and sex education. Education in itself is something good and to be valued. So one can deceive oneself, and under the pretext of seeking something good, actually seek only the gratification of his sensual appetite, and the satisfaction of the lust of the flesh.

Also, one must be on his guard against beginnings. "Beware of beginnings," it has been written by a holy writer. The first time one compromises and cheats in the area of chastity makes it easier to compromise the second time; and the second time leads to a third time, and finally a habit of impurity develops. A habit is something deeply rooted in one's nature and is very difficult to uproot. It has been said, "A fruit once tasted is always desired." With a realistic understanding of human nature, one should always be on his guard against this first bite, this first taste, and the beginning.

One must also be on guard against particular friendships in community life. "Beware of people," says Jesus. And St. Paul says, "Do not associate with evil persons." The human heart is so weak and the emotions so fragile that it is so very easy to become emotionally attached to another person, even of the same sex.

The criterium by which one judges any friendship is Christ. Does this affection, this friendship, this love draw me closer to Jesus, or does it draw me away from Him? Only if it draws me closer to Jesus is it good and do I preserve it. If in any way it weakens my love for Jesus and separates me from Him, I must break it ruthlessly and immediately. A particular friendship also violates brotherly love. It is all absorbing and creates jealousy, dissension, and division in a community, and quickly becomes a scandal to others. It very easily leads to little compromises in the area of chastity.

A particular friendship is similar to infatuation with a member of the opposite sex. One who is emotionally involved always thinks of the lover, wishes to be close to him, is extremely happy when he is nearby, speaks to him without reserve of all the secrets of his life and heart, and shows his affection by many little looks, expressions, words, gifts, and touches.

It is not enough to avoid particular friendships, but we must also avoid the appearance of a particular friendship or emotional involvement. It is not enough to avoid evil, but also the appearance of evil. One must always strengthen the faith of those about one and give witness to Christ by example. One can pretend there is no emotional involvement; but if one gives the impression of emotional involvement and others misunderstand a certain relationship, then this too must be corrected and rectified.

In a similar manner, one should avoid special attachment to children under one's care. Human nature is so weak and our emotions are so sensitive that it is quite easy to become attached even to a child. This attachment, also, can lead to emotional, sensual, even sexual temptation and involvement.

In the Gospel, Jesus says, "If your eye, or your hand cause you to sin, pluck out your eye and cut off your hand." In a similar manner, emotional involvement requires radical surgery. One should separate cleanly and clearly from the child to whom one is emotionally attached. One should courageously call the matter to the attention of one's superior, and quietly ask that the child be placed under the care of another sister. One should not hesitate, nor delay, nor procrastinate. It is very easy to become emotionally attached and involved. It is very difficult to become unattached and uninvolved; but one must treat such a matter courageously, forcefully, and uncompromisingly.

The devil loves a heart which is troubled, uneasy, anxious, and full of free-flowing guilt, especially in the area of past mistakes concerning chastity. The devil constantly tries to disturb one's inner peace, calm, and serenity. But God does not like a heart which is anxious, a heart which is troubled. We must totally believe in God's mercy, compassion, and forgiveness especially in the area of chastity. After Jesus forgave Mary Magdalene and cast from her seven devils, she never looked back with a sense of guilt or inferiority. She was Jesus' closest friend; and it is remarkable to see the child-like simplicity and natural affection which characterized her relationship with Jesus. There is no sense of awkwardness, shame, or lingering guilt. She trusted completely in the mercy and forgiveness of Jesus.

It is written in the Psalms, "The Lord knows of what we are made and that we are made only of dust, of clay." God knows our weakness -- especially in the areas of sins of the flesh. He forgives easily; and after He forgives, in a sense, He forgets. It is written in the Psalms, "The Lord says, I cast your sins behind my back." And again it is written, "Charity covers a multitude of sins." And "Charity does not remember evil." God is infinite charity, and in His infinite love, He covers our weaknesses and forgets our mistakes. So, too, must we. We must rid our heart of any lingering sense of guilt. This only makes us tense, depressed, sad, and prevents us from responding fully to the love of Jesus. It is also an impediment to the practice of brotherly love and the service of the poor.

The Patroness of the Sisters of Mary is Our Lady of Banneux, who introduces herself to the child, as the "Virgin of the Poor." Mary chooses this title deliberately. It is a title of honor.

The vocation of the Sister of Mary is also to be a "virgin of the poor." The Sisters of Mary serve the poor as virgins. They also have a special obligation, not only to practice chastity, but to bear witness to chastity and to teach chastity to others by word and example -- especially to the children entrusted to them.

In order to bear effective witness to chastity we must manifest the joy, happiness, and peace which is found in a life of true chastity. Many religious and priests, in a sense, do not properly digest chastity; and so it is, they always look like they are suffering indigestion. There is a sense of sadness, repression, and frustration about them. If we go about like an old man, dried up, bitter, and sad, it is very difficult to say with conviction, "Blessed are the pure of heart."

The "Virgin of the Poor" is a smiling virgin, she is clothed in radiant garments, clothed in light. So, too, by our constant, spiritual joy, happiness, cheerfulness, and childlikeness, we must give effective witness to the virtue of chastity.

CHAPTER 9

JESUS, OBEDIENT EVEN UNTO DEATH

By the vow of obedience the Sister of Mary promises to imitate Jesus in His spirit of obedience.

This spirit of absolute, unconditional, blind obedience is the most outstanding characteristic of Jesus.

St. Paul speaks of the mind and the spirit of Jesus in terms of obedience in his Epistle to the Philippians. St. Paul writes, "My brothers, have in you the same mind that was in Christ Jesus. Although equal to God, He did not cling to this equality. He lowered Himself. He emptied Himself. He took on the form of a slave. He was obedient, obedient even unto death on the cross."

Again in his Epistle to the Hebrews, St. Paul speaks of the sacrifice of Jesus as essentially a sacrifice of obedience. St. Paul writes, "Sacrifice and oblation I do not desire, says the Lord. But it is written of me, I come to do your will."

Isaiah the Prophet, seven hundred years before the coming of Christ, describes him also in terms of obedience. Isaiah speaks of the Savior who is to come as, "the suffering servant of Yahweh." A servant or a slave is the ultimate symbol of blind and absolute obedience. At the time of Isaiah, the servant or slave belonged totally -- body and soul -- to his lord and master. The master could treat the slave as an animal. He could abuse him, use him, beat him, and even kill him; and this was in no way a violation of the law. The role of the servant or slave was to do, always and only, what the lord and master instructed him to do. Jesus then is the servant and slave of Yahweh. He not only obeys, He obeys in suffering, humiliation, and death.

In the Gospels, Jesus repeatedly describes Himself in terms of obedience. He says, for example, "I do always the things which please My Father." Again, "My food is to do the will of Him who sent Me and to accomplish His work." In another place, Jesus says, "I have come not to do my own will but that of my Father."

There is something almost compulsive, obsessive, and imperative in the spirit of obedience which Jesus manifests. For example, He is in a village of Samaria where He wins the favor of the people. They wish Him to remain with them and to rest, relax, and enjoy their hospitality. Jesus objects strongly and says, "I must go to all the other villages of Palestine and there too I must announce the good news of salvation." It is not something which Jesus would like to do, or that He is free to do. It is an absolute imperative; that is, it is something which He must do because it is the will of the Father. This is why He was sent, and this is why He has come.

Here is another example of this almost obsessive spirit of obedience. When Jesus was in Galilee someone ran to Him, warned Him to vacate the premises immediately because the soldiers of Herod were seeking to kill Him. He was in mortal danger if He remained there and continued preaching. Jesus dismissed the threat with the words, "You go and tell that fox that today, tomorrow, and the next day, I must go My way." Again, Jesus speaks in terms of an absolute imperative. "No matter what the danger, no matter what the sacrifice, and no matter what the opposition, I must continue to preach the Gospel, because this is the will of My Father, My Lord and Master."

In the Gospels it is significant that the only prayer which Jesus teaches His disciples is essentially a prayer of obedience. "When you pray," Jesus instructs, "say Father." To call God, "Father," you must have the spirit of a child which is one of surrender, abandonment, and obedience to the Father. He goes on to say, "Thy name be glorified. Thy kingdom come. Thy will be done." We must pray to the Father, as did Jesus, with the spirit of a child, the spirit of a servant, and a slave -- which is to say, a spirit of humble faith, total abandonment, and complete obedience.

Obedience is not only the outstanding feature of Jesus, it is also the most salient characteristic of Mary, His mother. Mary listens to the words of the angel; but she does not grasp their meaning, nor does she understand fully their implication. But one thing is clear: this is the will of the Father. So Mary does not hesitate. She answers immediately in a spirit of total abandonment and child-like obedience. She says, "Behold the servant of the Lord. Be it done unto me according to thy word."

Mary, following the instructions of the angel, in a spirit of lighthearted, cheerful, child-like obedience, runs to her cousin, Elizabeth. Elizabeth greets Mary. Under impulse of the Holy Spirit she praises Mary and says, "You are the most favored and blessed among all women. Why? Because you have believed." Mary's belief is an "action belief." It is a belief which is proven by the sacrifice of her will, and the sacrifice of obedience. In the Gospels, the words "obedience," "faith," "child-likeness," and "trust," are used almost interchangeably. They are words which describe one and the same mind, spirit, and attitude.

Mary sings the song, called the "Magnificat," which is really a hymn to obedience. Mary says, "The Lord has looked with favor on the lowliness of His servant. He who is mighty has done great things to me." Mary understands that in humble, trusting, and child-like obedience is found the marvelous power of God. When she is most humble, she is most powerful. When she is most obedient, she is most pleasing to God.

At the wedding feast of Cana, again through Mary, we see dramatized the spirit of obedience which makes us most pleasing to God and most powerful in a spiritual way. Mary, together with Jesus and His disciples, attend the wedding banquet at Cana. The wine gives out. Mary notices the lack of wine. Immediately, she takes the initiative, goes to Jesus, and entrusts to Him the problem at hand. She says, "They have no wine." The reply of Jesus seems curt and cold: "Woman, what business is this of mine? My hour has not yet come." Mary is not offended. She humbles herself, calls the servants, and pointing to Jesus, she says, "Do whatever He tells you to do."

Jesus tells the servants to do something which to their way of thinking, does not make much sense. He tells them to fill the six water jugs with water. This is not a simple task, because each jug contains about 25 gallons. The servants know there is no need of water but

that it is wine which is lacking. Yet, they do blindly
what Jesus tells them to do; they obey unconditionally.
They take the water jugs to the chief steward who tastes,
and discovers that the water has been turned into wine --
the most precious, valuable, and delicious wine.

This is the first miracle which Jesus performs in the
Gospels. It is really a "miracle of obedience." We see
clearly, once again, the marvelous power hidden in this
humble, blind, and child-like spirit of obedience.

The Sister of Mary should meditate on this lesson at
Cana and try to imitate Mary and the servants in their
spirit of obedience. The Sister of Mary imagines Mary,
the Mother of Jesus, pointing to the representative of
Jesus, her superior, and saying, "Do whatever He tells
you to do." Even if the Sister of Mary does not
understand what is commanded, as was the case with
the servants, if she obeys joyfully, blindly, and
completely she will see marvels of grace and miracles of
goodness.

By the vow of obedience we offer to the Father our
most precious possession, our free will. This is the
sacrifice which pleases Him the most, and which
obtains for us the most blessings and graces. By the vow
of poverty we sacrifice material possessions through
Jesus to the Father. By the vow of chastity we sacrifice
physical pleasure and offer our bodies as living
sacrifices through Jesus to the Father. By the vow of
service we sacrifice our time, our energy, our life's
blood, and offer this for the poor through Jesus to the
Father. By the vow of prayer we offer a daily sacrifice of
praise through Jesus to the Father. But by the vow of
obedience we break, crush, and renounce our will; we
nail our will to the cross with Jesus, and offer it through
Him to the Father. This is the greatest renunciation, the
most difficult sacrifice, and this above all is what
redeems the world and sanctifies souls.

"In unity there is strength." The vow of obedience
unites hearts and wills; and in this union, strength to
serve the poor is dramatically increased and
geometrically multiplied. The Sisters whose wills and
hearts are united in Jesus in a spirit of humble
obedience have more strength and power for good than a
thousand individuals who are essentially following their

own will and living by their own commands and instructions.

"Divide and conquer," goes the maxim. This is the tactic of the devil, who in the words of St. Paul, is "a spirit of fornication and division." The devil tries to dissipate the strength of the servants of God by sowing the seeds of division through a spirit of proud disobedience. We see this spirit of disobedience in hell where the atmosphere is one of total chaos, disorder, division, and disharmony. Each soul in hell is there because of proud disobedience and the worship of his own individual will as a private idol and separate god.

But -- in the words of St. Paul -- "Our God is a God not of disorder, but of order." He is a God of peace. This peace, order, and harmony of God are found in child-like obedience.

In the Gospel Jesus says, "A house divided against itself cannot stand, it will fall, crumble, and collapse." And so it is that any religious community which is divided by a spirit of disobedience will not endure.

The bedrock on which is founded the Sisters of Mary is obedience. They will stand or fall by their spirit of obedience.

Many outsiders look at the Sisters of Mary and express concern about the future. They ask the question, "What will happen when your founder dies?"

The founder will live on if the Sister in her heart has this spirit of child-like obedience. Even if he is separated physically from the community, he will be alive and active in this spirit of continuing, joyful, and trusting obedience.

The survival of the Sisters of Mary as a community which serves the poor in the name of Christ depends essentially on the observance of this vow and the practice of this virtue of obedience. The foundation of the Sisters of Mary is not money, nor is it constitutions, rules, regulations, and books of spirituality, and prayers. It does not matter whether the Sisters have local, diocesan approval, or pontifical approval. These do not determine their continuation as a community and a family. The one thing which does determine their continuation is the

spirit of humble, trusting, and child-like obedience --
obedience even unto death.

The Sister of Mary strives to obey, not just externally
but internally as well. Her obedience is accompanied by
love. She gives through her founder and superior to
Jesus, not only her will, but her heart. She tries to make
the judgments of the founder her own judgments. She
tries to embrace his decisions, his thoughts, and make
them her own. Along these lines, in her heart she
refrains from negative criticism, judgmental thinking,
and fault finding. She is careful to refrain from saying
anything that will weaken the respect, loyalty, and
devotion of their fellow sisters to the founder and
superior.

"God chooses," according to the words of St. Paul,
"what is weak, what is foolish, what is powerless. He
chooses things which are weak, rejected, and lowly." In
this sense, God has chosen the founder and He makes
him His instrument. "God speaks to man through
man." He speaks to us through the founder who seeks
only what pleases Jesus, what is His will, and what are
His desires. In the spirit of faith, we do not look for the
faults, defects, mistakes, and failures of the founder;
rather, we try to see in him the living Christ. We open
the ears of our hearts and we say, as did Samuel in the
Old Testament, "Speak Lord, your servant listens." And
the Lord will speak to us through the founder. We try to
accept his words as the words of Jesus, and we do our
best to obey and follow him -- even when we do not fully
comprehend or understand.

The obedience of the Sister of Mary should be modeled
after that of Mary. Her obedience was joyful,
lighthearted, and child-like. Mary, at the instructions of
the angel, immediately left her home in Nazareth and
ran to her cousin Elizabeth, and sang the song called the
Magnificat. This is the obedience we try to emulate.
Singing in our hearts, we obey lightly, joyfully, and in a
child-like manner -- not reluctantly, mechanically, nor
in a militaristic manner. In the words of St. Paul, "God
loves a cheerful giver."

The obedience of the Sister of Mary is a dynamic,
active, moving, thinking, living, anticipatory obedience.
We do not strive to obey as a cadaver or a stick. On the

contrary, we take the initiative, we take responsibility, we are always alert, alive, and thinking; and so it is we always have constructive advice, suggestions, and ideas to offer to those in charge and in positions of authority.

The model for this type of obedience, again, is found in Mary. At the wedding feast of Cana, she saw the wine had given out. She did not shrug her shoulders and say, "What does it matter?" On the contrary, she immediately took the initiative. She presented the matter to Jesus; and, although Jesus apparently rebuked her, she continued to pursue the matter until she obtained this marvelous miracle of grace whereby water was changed into wine.

"Whosoever is a little one, let him come unto me," says the Lord. Child-like, lowly, and humble obedience is the short cut to God. It is the way of the Lord, and it is the path that leads to the peak of the mountain of perfection.

Obedience, then, is the bedrock upon which is founded the Sisters of Mary. As long as this spirit of obedience remains dynamic, humble, sacrificial, and alive, the Sisters of Mary will continue to stand and resist all the winds and storms which beat against them and try to bring them down. If this spirit of obedience -- in imitation of Jesus and Mary -- continues forever, so too will the Sisters of Mary.

CHAPTER 10

SERVING THE POOR IN THE NAME OF CHRIST

By the vow of service the Sister of Mary promises to serve the poor in the name of Christ -- which is to say, with the mind, heart, and spirit of Christ.

Christ-like service of the poor has three primary characteristics. It is self-sacrificing; it is humble; and it is above all spiritual.

In the Gospel Jesus says, "I have come to serve." And immediately he adds, "I have come to give my life as a ransom for many." We see then that these two ideas of service and sacrifice are intimately related in the mind, teaching, and life of Christ.

Isaiah the Prophet speaks of this quality of sacrifice in the service of Christ when he writes, "He was wounded with our wounds and thus He healed us." Jesus is the Divine Physician. His manner of relieving pain and treating sickness is totally new. The Divine Physician assumes in His own flesh the suffering, sickness, and pain of the patient, and in so doing heals him, and restores him to health, vigor, and life.

In this same spirit, Jesus in the Gospel says, "No greater love has any man than this, that he lay down his life for his friends." Jesus declares the poor, the lowly, and the suffering to be His special friends. He comes for all men but especially for these little ones. What is more, He comes to offer His life, especially for these poor, downtrodden, and neglected people.

St. Paul expresses the same idea in his Second Epistle to the Corinthians where he writes, "Jesus Christ being rich, became poor for our sakes, so that by His poverty we might become rich."

Before Jesus came to earth He was living in heaven very much as the rich man in the parable of Lazarus and Dives. As Dives, Jesus in heaven was in a sense clothed in rich garments and was feasting sumptuously every day. He possessed all things, enjoyed infinite happiness, and had access to every pleasure. Nothing was lacking to him. Jesus in heaven, seated at His Father's banquet table, looked towards the gate and saw Lazarus lying there. Lazarus was a pitiful sight indeed. He was covered with sores as a leper -- starving, rejected, dying. Only the dogs who came to lick his wounds took any interest in him. Lazarus is a symbol of every man -- you and me before the coming of Jesus. In a spiritual sense each one of us was every bit as pitiful, helpless, and neglected.

Jesus takes pity on Lazarus, and out of overflowing love wishes to help him. Jesus can help Lazarus simply by snapping his fingers, summoning his servants -- the angels -- and instructing them to go and help that poor creature lying there at my Father's gate. In other words, Jesus could have helped Lazarus without bruising his body, shedding his blood, or sacrificing his life. But in the words of St. Paul, "The love of Christ is long-suffering," -- which is to say, it is a love based on sacrifice and renunciation. So Jesus leaves His Father's house, goes to Lazarus, and changes places with him. Jesus becomes the beggar covered with sores -- suffering, starving, and dying. And Lazarus is now clothed in rich garments, seated at the Father's table, enjoying a sumptuous banquet.

In the story of the Good Samaritan, Jesus reveals His mode of service in a very simple, clear, and dramatic manner. The Good Samaritan is the model of Christ-like service of the poor. And the salient feature of His service is self-sacrifice.

The Samaritan sees a stranger lying by the side of the road who is naked, bleeding, unconscious, and half dead. The stranger is also a Jew -- a sworn enemy of the Samaritans. The Samaritan cannot help but be repelled by the sight of this naked, bleeding, pitiful stranger who is also an enemy from way back. But the Samaritan goes against his natural inclination to ignore what he sees and hurry by. He sacrifices emotionally and psychologically, and although he feels no attraction, he goes to this stranger -- this Jew and enemy -- and he serves him and helps him as if it were his own flesh and blood.

The Samaritan who is apparently on a business trip also gives and sacrifices his precious time. He sacrifices his strength and energy as well, by serving and helping with his own hands. He treats and bandages the wounds of the unfortunate stranger. He puts the man on his own beast and takes him to the inn. The Samaritan further sacrifices his sleep for the wounded stranger and watches with him all night. In the morning he sacrifices his money and gives generously to the innkeeper what is necessary to continue proper care and treatment of the ailing man. Jesus concludes the story with the call to action, "You too go and do likewise." It is clear, then, if one wishes to serve as did the Good Samaritan, one must have the willingness and the courage to sacrifice.

We see this spirit of sacrifice manifested in the lives of many saints who were models and heroes of service. For example, St. John Bosco loved the poor street boys entrusted to his care. At night he would walk through the dormitories in which they were sleeping. Occasionally, he would come upon a lad who was suffering a toothache or headache, and he would pray for the boy. But his prayer was not the usual prayer, "Dear God, take care of this little lad and relieve him of his suffering." John Bosco prayed in a different manner, "Dear God give me this toothache, this headache, or this stomachache, and relieve the suffering of my youngsters." On many occasions God took him at his word and answered his prayer literally. The boy in question would be relieved of his ailment; and instead, Don Bosco's tooth would begin to ache, his head throb, or his stomach hurt.

Another well-known example of Christ-like service to the poor can be found in the life of Father Damien of Molokai. Father Damien not only helped the poor lepers, but also, he went to them, lived with them, became one of them, and eventually died a leper.

The most common mistake made by those who wish to serve the poor is that they want to do this without stubbing a toe, bruising a finger, or shedding a single drop of blood. So many want the sense of fulfillment which comes from effectively helping the poor, but they want this without any pain, suffering or discomfort whatsoever. This is very much against the spirit of Christ and the teaching of the Gospels.

Jesus says, "Unless the grain of wheat falls into the ground and dies, it remains alone and will bear no fruit." Death is a symbol of supreme sacrifice and absolute renunciation. Unless one is willing to suffer and die, one cannot expect to reap the fruits of Christ-like service and love of the poor.

St. Paul in one of his Epistles writes, "In the cross there is salvation, life, and resurrection." The goal of Christ-like service of the poor is precisely this; namely, the giving of salvation or health, life or vigor, resurrection or new hope and joy. This goal can be attained only if one believes in the cross, loves the cross, and is willing to deny himself and take up the cross every day.

It is obvious, then, that to make and keep the fourth vow of service of the poor requires great courage, strength, patience, perseverance, and determination. To serve the poor in the name of Christ is not a game, it is not play acting, nor is it child's play. It means constant pain, discomfort, humiliation, suffering, and sacrifice. In a word, it means the cross.

The second primary attribute of Christ-like service of the poor is humility. In the Gospel Jesus says, "When you give alms to the poor -- in other words, when you serve the needy -- do not do it like the Pharisees. They sound a trumpet and do it in order to show off and be seen and praised by men." Jesus goes on to say, "When you give alms or help the poor, do it secretly for God and God alone. Do it quietly and humbly with a low profile. Do it in such a way that even your left hand does not know what your right hand is doing."

Jesus Himself gives an example of this humble and low-profile service in the Gospels. He performs a great miracle of service when He multiplies the loaves and fishes and feeds a huge crowd of hungry people. The poor people after eating become excited and enthusiastic. They rush at Jesus to praise, applaud, and exalt Him. What is Jesus' reaction? He flees. This flight of Jesus from the praise, glory, and recognition of men is meant to teach us an important lesson. We should also hold in contempt the praise and glory of the world, and serve the poor, and help the needy for God and God alone. In the Gospel Jesus says, "What men hold in esteem, God mightily despises." What men hold most in esteem is the esteem of their fellow men. God despises this, and in a spirit of faith so too must we when we serve the poor and help the needy.

In this spirit St. Paul writes, "Whether you eat, whether you drink, whatsoever else you do, do all for the glory of God." And again, "In word, in deed, whatever you do, do all in the name of Christ."

In the Psalms we read the words "Not to us, oh Lord, not to us, but to Thy name alone give glory." In the writings of Isaiah, the Prophet, we read these words, "It is the Lord who has accomplished all that I have done." If we do any good or accomplish anything worthwhile for the poor we must realize that of and by ourselves we can accomplish no lasting good. If anything good is accomplished through our efforts, it is a result of God's grace, help, and assistance.

The parable of the Good Samaritan ends with the Samaritan fading from the scene in silence. There is no mention of praise, glory, recognition, or a reward of any type whatsoever. The Samaritan serves the man set upon by robbers in a quiet, hidden, and humble manner. And Jesus says, "You, too, go and do in like manner."

The third basic quality of Christ-like service is its spiritual dimension. Christ-like service of the poor is neither materialistic, worldly, nor physical; rather it is primarily spiritual. And above all it is based on faith.

In the Gospel of St. Matthew we read the account of the angel who appears to Joseph in a dream. The angel speaks of the child who is in Mary's womb. And the angel says, "His name shall be called Jesus, which means savior. He will save the people from sin." Jesus, the savior, comes then to save the people not from poverty, sickness, ignorance, nor physical oppression, but above all from sin. Jesus comes first and foremost to save the souls of the poor. "To save souls" is an expression which is now out of vogue in the Church, but it has a depth of meaning. "To save a soul" means to give an individual eternal life, and this is the highest expression of love and the most sublime form of charity imaginable. Eternal life means happiness, which is full, complete, perfect, and above all, everlasting. There is no greater good nor is there anything more desirable than this. And this is the object and the ultimate goal of Christ-like service of the poor.

In the Gospels, Christ's outlook was unrelentingly spiritual. He saw all things in the light of eternity. His emphasis was always on the other world, the world of God, the invisible world of faith. At times Christ seems totally unrealistic, and at times almost fanatical in His emphasis on the spiritual.

For example, Christ says, "Do not be concerned with what you shall eat, drink, or wear. The pagans seek these things. You must seek God and His kingdom, and He will give all of these things and more besides." Again Jesus says, "The flesh avails nothing, it is the spirit which gives life." And still again, "What does it profit a man if he gain the whole world and suffer the loss of his own soul?"

Jesus emphasizes this spiritual dimension in His message in the parable of the rich farmer. The farmer, in a worldly sense, was extremely successful. To enjoy life even more, he decided to tear down his barns and build new, bigger, and better ones. He decided to eat, drink, and enjoy. People of the world look upon such a one as highly successful, and frequently such a one becomes a role model for the poor, the lowly, the downtrodden, and the destitute. But God looks at this rich, successful farmer and calls him a "fool." He was a fool because he lived, acted, and made plans as if this world were forever. He had no thought of the life after death -- a life which is eternal. We too are fools indeed if we serve the poor with the outlook of the rich farmer -- the outlook of the materialist, the hedonist, and the man of this world. If we love the poor in Christ, we wish to give them the very best, the greatest, and the most sublime gift imaginable; namely, eternal happiness.

In the Gospel, it is not only by word but by action as well that Jesus stresses this spiritual and other-worldly quality of His service. One day Jesus comes upon a multitude of poor people. He takes pity upon them, and He goes to them. He does not give them money, food, clothing, medicine, or shelter -- but He gives them truth. In the words of the Gospel Jesus begins to teach them. And what does He teach them? Basically, He teaches them the way of God, the way to eternal happiness -- the way to save their souls.

St. Thomas Aquinas has written, "The greatest charity is the giving of truth." After giving these poor people truth, Jesus then heals the sick. He does this only afterwards, thereby clearly indicating what are His priorities.

On another occasion a paralytic is brought to Jesus. Jesus looks at the man with pity and says, "Your sins are forgiven you." The man must have been crestfallen. He was not thinking of his sins, nor of his soul, but primarily of his body and his physical infirmity. After Jesus heals the man's soul, then and only then, does He turn His attention to his body. Then Jesus says, "Take up thy pallet and walk." Here again by deed Jesus gives us a lesson. He tells us by this miracle that it serves no purpose to heal the body while the soul is still sick, ailing, and suffering.

People of the world tend to look upon service of the poor which emphasizes the spiritual as being narrow, restricted, and very limited. But the opposite is true. Spiritual service of the poor is as wide, broad, and open as eternity and infinitude. It is service that has the full dimension and completeness of perfect love. In the Gospel Jesus says, "I come that my sheep may have life, and that they may have it in abundance." The "sheep" of Jesus, are above all, the poor, the needy, and the little ones. The "abundant life" which Jesus comes to give is eternal life in God, eternal happiness, and salvation.

Besides the primary attributes of sacrifice, humility, and spirituality, Christ-like service of the poor has a number of secondary attributes, most of which are brought out in the parable of the Good Samaritan.

The Good Samaritan sees the stranger lying by the side of the road he "takes pity on him." In other words, the Samaritan serves the stranger not simply out of a sense of duty, mechanically, or reluctantly; but he serves him with pity, with gentleness, with tenderness, with warmth, with heart and passion. Christ-like service of the poor, in a word, is service with a smile.

In the Gospel when Jesus saw the multitude of poor people who were wandering about as sheep without a shepherd, Jesus, too, "took pity on them." Jesus went to them and served them with great warmth, gentleness, tenderness, and respect.

On another occasion in the Gospel, Jesus stands before the multitude of poor people and says to them with a smile, "Come to me all you who labor and are heavily burdened, and I will refresh you." Again with the same gentle smile, Jesus says, "Suffer the little children to come unto me and prevent them not." Upon saying this He takes each of these children -- children of the poor -- one by one in His arms, then caresses and blesses each child. In other words, Jesus shows individual respect for each child. Jesus says, "Take care and do not despise even one of these little ones." Basically, Jesus teaches us that we are to serve and treat the poor as close, intimate, and personal friends.

As seen in the story of the Good Samaritan, Christ-like service of the poor is also direct, personal, and hands-on service. The Samaritan in the story does not call a passerby, as perhaps he could have done, give him money, and instruct him to take care of the unconscious stranger lying there by the side of the road. He goes himself and serves. He helps directly, personally, with his own hands. In the Gospel at the Last Supper Jesus does the same. With His own hands He personally washes and dries the feet of His disciples. He concludes by saying, "As you have seen me do, so too must you do to each other."

Most frequently in the Gospels, when Jesus heals and helps He goes directly to the person in need and touches Him -- even when that person is as repulsive as a leper. Jesus shows His personal respect for the individual in need by His personal, direct, hands-on service and healing.

Also in the parable of the Good Samaritan, we can deduce that service in the spirit of Christ is quality service. It is service which is complete, modern, and result-oriented. The Samaritan gave the stranger the best service possible according to the custom and wisdom of the day. He did not simply go to the stranger, hold his hand, wipe his brow, and wait for him to die. He served the stranger as best he could, as if it were a question of his own flesh and blood. He used medicine, bandaged the wounds of the stranger, nursed the man, and watched with him all night. There was also a follow-up. After giving the money to the innkeeper, the Samaritan said that on his way back he would pay any other expenses which the innkeeper had incurred. In other words, he would check up on the man and make sure that his recovery was full and complete.

Too many people labor under the fallacy that just because the person being helped is poor, lowly, and needy, anything goes. Too frequently the poor are given the worst quality service. But in God's scheme of things the poor are the VIPs: they have priority in His love and first claim to His heart. Jesus comes, first and foremost, to announce the Gospels to the poor, and to liberate the oppressed, the suffering, and the little ones. With this in mind, it is not fitting nor is it Christ-like to serve the poor in a mediocre, or perfunctory manner. We must serve them with the most modern techniques available, give them the best treatment possible, and try to achieve lasting results.

In the Gospels Jesus Himself was a one-man-medical service team for the poor and the needy, and the service He offered was the best imaginable. When Jesus healed the sick, they stayed healed. When He cured the ailing, their recovery was complete and permanent. In other words His medical program was the highest quality and the very best imaginable. Along the same lines, when Jesus makes wine out of water, He makes wine of the very best quality. When He multiplies the loaves and fishes, He does this in a magnanimous manner and distributes them most generously. After the people ate and were satisfied, they gathered up what remained and filled twelve baskets. All these events, directly and indirectly, reveal the mind and heart of Christ and His modus operandi. We see that Christ is very much the realist and the man of action, who is very "result-oriented." We too must try to inculcate these qualities in our service of the poor.

Christ-like service of the poor is also free. After the Good Samaritan took care of the man set upon by robbers, there was no talk of the man paying him back in any manner or form. No money changes hands, except the money which the Samaritan gives to the innkeeper. In the Gospels, Christ helps and serves in the same style. For example, after He distributes the loaves and fishes, there are no kickbacks. After Jesus heals the sick, neither He nor His apostles demand a fee for His services.

There is a prevailing wisdom which says that you never give anything free to the poor. Why? Well, everyone knows that you will only spoil them and make parasites out of them. But in the Gospels, Christ's service was totally free. God's grace is also totally free. There is no merit on our part at all. And Jesus says, "Freely have you received, freely give." Free, no-strings-attached service of the poor and the needy is very much in accord with the spirit of the Gospels. In a sense, it is also a symbol of God's grace and God's manner of giving His blessings to us.

There is one final lesson that can be drawn from the story of the Good Samaritan. The Samaritan is the hero of this story of service, yet, he is a heretic. The priest and deacon who were accepted members of the established church are the villains of the piece. Members of the institutional church of that day and age, the priest and deacon looked down upon the Samaritan and considered him an outcast and an outlaw. Yet Jesus indirectly teaches us that it is the Samaritan -- and not the priest and the deacon -- who are closest to God. The priest and the deacon are "material" heretics. By their actions they show that they do not believe in the priority of love, the importance of mercy, and the necessity of service in God's design and plan. On the other hand, the Samaritan, although considered a "formal" heretic, shows by his action that he is the one who is really orthodox and in tune with the spirit of Christ and message of the Gospels.

Christ concludes the story of the Good Samaritan with the simple injunction, "Go and do in like manner." Christ does not add the admonition, "Provided of course, those in authority fully approve, sanction, and support what you are doing."

Frequently, the saints and heroes of service found themselves in conflict with those in positions of authority. One example which comes to mind is St. John Bosco. For fully seventeen years, he suffered misunderstanding and opposition from his bishop. Frequently, John Bosco would come away from meetings with his bishop in tears. To such an extent was John Bosco misunderstood that during one year of his priestly life, he was suspended from hearing confessions.

Another example is that of St. Vincent de Paul. His Daughters of Charity, although model servants of the poor, were not accepted as "religious" by church authorities, nor were they permitted to wear official religious garb. St. Vincent's Daughters of Charity went out to serve dressed in lay attire, and they called themselves a "company" -- rather than a religious order or congregation.

Jesus says, "By their fruits you shall know them." If a given group which serves the poor bears fruit which is 1) abundant, 2) high quality, and 3) continuous, one can conclude that such a group is inspired and impelled by the Holy Spirit and is sanctioned and approved by the highest authority, God Himself.

In conclusion, service in the name of Christ implies self-sacrifice, humility, and a spiritual dimension. Furthermore, Christ-like service is kind, direct, personal, free, modern, and result-oriented.

CHAPTER 11

PRAY ALWAYS AND NEVER GROW WEARY

The Sister of Mary takes a fifth vow to pray about three hours a day in imitation of Jesus on the Cross.

The word "about" is significant. It reminds us that we must not interpret this vow in a strict, scrupulous, or pharisaical manner. It means we try our best each day to put in about three hours of formal prayer. If on some days we are exceptionally busy and cannot find the time, we are not unduly upset. We merely try to fill up the lack by putting in more time on other days when we have more leisure. For example, our days of recollection and retreat enable us to make up any shortfall which may occur in our daily prayer life.

This fifth vow of prayer is really the foundation of the fourth vow to serve the poor in the name of Christ. In the Gospel Jesus says, "Without me you can do nothing." Without prayer, we are without Jesus. We are on our own, and we work and serve alone. Such work will be fruitless, and such service will be ineffective.

In the Gospels, Jesus Himself gives us a forceful lesson concerning the fundamental necessity of prayer. Jesus comes to earth basically to serve the poor and to give His life as a ransom, especially for them. His three years of public life were years of self-sacrificing service, especially of the poor. However, before embarking on this life of service, Jesus goes into the desert and prays for 40 days and 40 nights. Then He comes out and begins to serve.

The lesson is clear: Only if we pray as Jesus prayed, can we serve the poor as Jesus served them.

Again, in the tenth chapter in the Gospel of St. Luke, we have an eloquent lesson in the priority of prayer. In this chapter we read the parable of the Good Samaritan. Jesus concludes this lesson in service with the words, "You, too, go and do in like manner." This parable is followed immediately by the account of Jesus' visit to the home of Martha in Bethany. Jesus speaks to Martha these words, "Martha, Martha, you are worried and troubled by many things but not many things are necessary, only one. Mary has chosen the better part and it shall not be taken from her."

Mary, under the impulse of the Holy Spirit, had chosen the part of prayer. Seated at the feet of Jesus, she was listening to His words with faith and looking into His face with love. In effect she was offering to Jesus her mind through meditation and her heart in contemplation. Jesus states that this is "the one thing necessary," and that this is "the better part."

St. Luke under the inspiration of the Holy Spirit juxtaposes these two accounts, the account of the Good Samaritan and the account of Martha and Mary. The meaning of this juxtaposition is clear: if you wish to serve the poor with the self-sacrificing spirit of the Good Samaritan, you must first imitate Mary in her spirit of prayer.

Again, in this same tenth chapter of St. Luke, Jesus says, "The first and the greatest commandment is this: you shall love the Lord your God with all your mind, your heart, your will, your strength." The first and greatest commandment is a commandment to pray. By prayer we go directly to God, and without any intermediary, we love Him, adore Him, and serve Him with all our mind, heart, will, and strength.

Then Jesus adds, "The second commandment is like unto this: you shall love your neighbor as yourself." The second commandment is a commandment to serve one's neighbor, one's brother, and the poor. This second commandment is based on and flows from the first. Only by keeping the first commandment to pray can we find the will, the strength, and the light to keep the second commandment to love and serve our neighbor, our brother, and the poor.

In prayer we receive the light, the wisdom, and the guidance of Jesus. We learn what we must do and how to do it in order to help the needy in a manner which is fruitful, effective, and lasting. In the Gospel of St. John it is written that Jesus not only knows man, but he knows in detail what is in each one of us. We do not know the poor, nor do we know man. In fact, we do not even know ourselves. Accordingly, with all the good will and the best intentions in the world, we cannot help our fellow man in a manner which is truly effective, productive, and lasting.

In the Gospels, we have several examples of this. We are familiar with the story of the woman suffering from an issue of blood for twelve years. According to the Gospel account, she went to many doctors. These doctors with all their skill and good will could do nothing for her. They truly wished to help this woman. But all they accomplished was to use up all her money, to take up all her time, and to leave her in a condition worse than before. This is frequently the case with those in the world who wish to help and serve the poor. Too frequently they botch the job and leave the poor in a condition worse than before. However, the suffering woman in the Gospel episode comes to Jesus. His power flows into her, and she is healed completely, perfectly, and permanently.

Another example of those who wished to help but failed to do so is found in the story of the young boy who was a deaf mute and also possessed by a devil. The father brings the boy to the disciples of Jesus. They take pity on the youngster, want to help him and heal him. But they accomplish nothing except to disappoint the father and to waste the time of all concerned. Then Jesus arrives on the scene. Immediately, he casts out the devil and heals the boy. Then Jesus tells His amazed apostles, "This kind of demon can be cast out only by prayer and penance." Through constant prayer, we not only receive the light and wisdom to serve the poor, but also the will and the strength to serve them.

In the Gospel, Jesus say, "Pray always and never grow weary." Only if we pray regularly will we not grow weary of doing good and become burned out in our efforts to work for the needy and the oppressed. St. Paul writes, "God stirs up within us the will -- and accomplishes the doing to serve the poor." In prayer, God stirs up within us the will, and through prayer He pours into our hearts the strength, energy, grace, and power to continue to serve them, to shed our blood for them, and to offer our lives for them.

Too many people work for the poor, give themselves to the poor, serve the poor, then eventually suffer what is called "burnout." In other words, they simply become bored, weary, and tired of doing good. "Burnout" never occurs in those whose service of the poor is based on a life of constant prayer.

In the Psalms we read the words of the Holy Spirit, "Run lightly in the way of the Lord." "The way of the Lord" is a way of service, charity, and love. We are called to run this way everyday -- lightly, joyfully and enthusiastically.

To be a champion runner -- especially a champion distance runner -- two things are necessary. First, one must train with great intensity, concentration, and energy. Secondly, one must balance this constant, strenuous training and output of energy with regular rest and relaxation. The most frequent mistake made by failed and frustrated runners is that of over-training. They run more and more, and pile up the mileage in an almost obsessive and compulsive manner. Frequently, they end up by suffering chronic fatigue, by injuring themselves, or by experiencing total "burn-out."

The same mistake can be made by those called to "run in the way of the Lord," which is the way of service. Constant self-sacrifice is demanded, but this must be balanced by regular intervals of prayer, which is a form of spiritual resting, relaxation, and renewal. In prayer our energy is restored, our will is renewed, our strength is rejuvenated. And we can continue to run lightly, joyfully, and zestfully in the way of service of the poor to the end.

In the Gospel, Jesus instructs His apostles to pray, not just three hours a day, but "always." It can be objected, then, that our vow of three hours of daily prayer is too limited.

However, we must distinguish between two forms of prayer: "high-intensity" prayer and "low-intensity" prayer. "High-intensity" prayer -- or formal prayer -- requires concentration, focus, and constant effort. We promise to put in about three hours a day of this "high-intensity" form of prayer.

However, there is another form of prayer which can be described as "low-intensity" prayer. This type of prayer is a quiet, gentle, effortless awareness of God's presence, a simple look of love at Jesus, the softly speaking of his name in the silence of one's heart, or a child-like smile in His direction. We can practice this form of prayer constantly, almost effortlessly, and uninterruptedly day and night.

In fact, Jesus Himself indicates that He always was filled with the presence of God, and worked, moved, lived, and breathed with the consciousness of the Father's loving presence. "I and the Father are one," says Jesus in the Gospel.

This "low-intensity" form of prayer can be compared to a devoted mother who is busy cleaning, cooking, and doing the laundry in a room where her child is resting in his crib. The mother is constantly aware of the presence of her child. Occasionally she looks at the child with love or softly calls his name. Now and then she approaches the child, smiles at the child, and touches him. At times she picks the child up, embraces, kisses him lightly, and then puts him back in his crib. If the mother awakes during the night, her first thought is of the child asleep close by in the same room. The mother's consciousness is always filled with a loving awareness of the presence of her child, but it is something easy, gentle, and effortless.

In a similar manner, our hearts should be filled with the consciousness of Jesus. At all times, we should be aware of the presence of this loving friend. We should think constantly of Jesus, call His name with love, look at Him gently, and speak to Him a few words in the silence of our hearts. Now and then we should reach out and touch Him, embrace Him, and kiss Him as the Spirit of prayer moves us. This form of "low-intensity" prayer should become second nature to us. It should be as easy as breathing in and breathing out. Prayer is the oxygen of the soul, and in prayer we -- so to speak -- breathe God; breathe Jesus, and inhale His divine energy.

Our "high-intensity" prayer requires concentration, effort, and focus. We can do this only for limited periods of time, because it produces a certain amount of strain and stress. But we balance these two types of prayer:

"high-intensity" prayer for about three hours a day, and "low-intensity" prayer constantly, uninterruptedly, day and night. In this way, we develop the habit of prayer. We become a "man of prayer" as Jesus. And only if we become a "man of prayer" can we truly become a "man for others," a man who gives himself to the needy, and a man who serves the poor in the name of Jesus.

In prayer we not only find the light, the will, and the energy to serve the poor, but prayer itself is a form of spiritual service of the poor. In the Gospel, Jesus prays, not for Himself because He has no need of prayer, but for all men -- especially for the poor. Today, Jesus, seated at the right hand of the Father in glory, intercedes for us, and day and night He prays for all men -- especially the poor. Mary, the Virgin of the Poor, appears to Mariette Beco at Banneux. This child is the symbol of the poor of all places and of all times. And Mary with the same mind and spirit of Jesus in the Gospels, says to the child, "I will pray for you."

Our prayer benefits not only us, but it also obtains grace, blessings, and gifts for the poor entrusted to our care. In prayer we offer our minds and hearts to God through Jesus. At the same time, we offer those who are in our minds and hearts; namely, the poor, the abandoned children, the sick, and the suffering who are entrusted to our care. And when God looks at us in prayer, He sees at the same time those for whom we are sacrificing our lives -- the poor, and the little ones. Whenever God gives us a grace in prayer, at the same time, He gives another grace through us to the poor who are with us in spirit.

It is not necessary to think of each poor person or to mention his or her name and needs specifically in prayer. Sister Elizabeth of the Trinity mentioned that she was frequently confused by so many requests for prayer which came to her from friends and acquaintances. She solved the problem, she writes, in the following way. She would go before God to pray. She would look first at God, then she would look at the friend or acquaintance who was requesting her help in prayer. Then she would look again at God, and remain with her gaze fixed quietly and gently on God.

We can learn from Sister Elizabeth of the Trinity the way we should remember the poor in our prayers. We go to God in prayer and we look at Him. Then, we glance at the poor entrusted to our care. Then we look at God again, and remain with our gaze fixed on God in faith and love.

Prayer is essentially a mystery of faith. It is an expression of humility at its deepest level and in its highest form. When Jesus was participating in the banquet at the home of Lazarus, Mary Magdalene went in with a jar of precious ointment. She broke the jar and poured the ointment on the feet of Jesus. The house was filled with the sweet aroma of this perfume. Judas took offense of Mary's action and protested, "Would it not have been better to sell this and give the money to the poor?" Jesus rebuked Judas and defended the action of Mary, which was an expression of her faith and love.

When we pray we imitate Mary. We offer, through Jesus to the Father, our precious time. We pour it on the feet of Jesus like a precious ointment. Viewed externally, it seems a waste. In prayer we give the impression of being idle and doing nothing. At times we might be tempted like Judas to sell this precious perfume of our time and give it to the poor through useful and productive work. But as Mary in the Gospel, we reject this temptation, and express our faith and love by doing the opposite.

Jesus on the cross of Calvary also gives us a powerful lesson in the value of prayer. For three hours in the darkness of Calvary, in intense pain and humiliation, Jesus remains nailed to the cross. He is immobile, totally disabled, and apparently powerless. Nailed to the cross Jesus does not heal, nor preach, nor perform any miracle. He simply offers to the Father -- along with his blood, sweat, and tears -- His prayer. And this is what redeems the world and saves mankind. St. John of the Cross wrote, "The greatest work in the history of the world was accomplished by Jesus during the three hours when He was nailed to the cross on Calvary."

When we pray three hours a day, we, in effect, are trying to follow the example of Jesus. We enter the darkness of Calvary, the night of faith. We are joined with Jesus and united to Him on the cross. And along with our blood, sweat, and tears, we offer to the Father our humble prayer. This is how we participate in the work of redemption and creation. This is how we truly serve, save, and help the poor, the needy, and the little ones.

In the Old Testament, it is written: "Prayer accompanied by tears is most pleasing to God." Prayer and "tears," that is, sacrifice, go together like body and soul, like flesh and blood. Prayer without "tears," that is, without sacrifice, is anemic, weak, lifeless, dead. In a word, it is not the prayer of Jesus.

In the Gospels whenever Jesus speaks a prayer, at the same time He usually speaks of sacrifice. For example, Jesus says, "Pray always and never grow weary." Again, "Take care and pray constantly." And yet again, "Watch and pray that you enter not into temptation." "Never grow weary," "take care," "watch," -- these words are an expression of the sacrifice, renunciation, and self-denial required for prayer.

During his public life, Jesus prayed constantly, and His constant prayer was usually accompanied by sacrifice. For example, Jesus goes into the desert to pray for 40 days and 40 nights. At the same time He denies His flesh, its satisfaction, and He fasts. Jesus goes to the mountain at night to pray. He denies Himself sleep, and in the darkness, silence, and solitude of the night He prays until dawn. In the Gospel, it is also recorded that Jesus rises early before all the others and goes off to a quiet and empty place to pray alone. In the Garden of Gethsemane Jesus falls to the ground, with His face pressed to the earth, trembling and sweating blood, He prays. Finally on the cross of Calvary, Jesus with His heart filled with the darkness of despair, and His body racked by excruciating pain, prays unto the end. The prayer of Jesus then is not based on feeling, emotion, nor self-gratification -- even in a spiritual sense. It is based on sacrifice, self-denial, and self-renunciation.

Prayer by itself can be compared to the burning charcoal used for Benediction of the Blessed Sacrament. Sacrifice can be compared to the grains of incense which the priest places on the charcoal. Together, the burning coal and the grains of incense, produce a beautiful fragrance and sweet aroma which rises up before the throne of God, gives Him pleasure, and brings down an abundance of grace and blessings.

We prepare best for a life of prayer by a life of habitual sacrifice, renunciation, and mortification. St. Ignatius of Loyola says, "If we practice constant mortification, when we come before God to pray He immediately appears, and we become instantly aware of His loving presence." To paraphrase St. Ignatius, one who constantly practices mortification in His daily life comes to the chapel, and, in a sense, all He has to do is press a button and God immediately appears.

Prayer itself is a form of sacrifice and renunciation. We must patiently endure the silence, solitude, boredom, monotony, dryness, and tedium of prayer. We in no way seek the consolation of God, but the "God of consolations." We should not concern ourselves with our feelings or our emotions. Too many people -- even good and pious people -- seek an emotional high, spiritual stimulation, or a titillating change of consciousness through prayer. This is not the way in which Jesus prayed, nor is this the way in which Jesus teaches prayer in the Gospels.

In the garden of Gethsemane, Jesus felt totally depressed, yet He prayed all the more fervently. On the cross He experienced utter desolation, but He continued to pray unto the end. It requires courage, determination, patience, and perseverance to pray three hours a day in the manner in which Jesus prayed.

In the Gospels, Jesus emphasizes the necessity of patience and perseverance in prayer. He tells the story of the poor widow who goes to the home of the judge who is frightening and intimidating. The poor widow in question does not give up; but she humbles herself, patiently waits, and eventually wears down the judge by her courageous perseverance, and receives the help she sought.

Again, Jesus tells the story of the visitor who arrives unexpectedly in the middle of the night. The master of the house has no food to give him. So in the night he leaves his house, goes next door, knocks, and calls the name of his neighbor. And in the night he continues to knock, to beg, and to wait patiently for help until it is finally given to him.

In the Psalms it is written, "God gives to His beloved even while they are asleep." Frequently in prayer our hearts are dry, and our senses are as asleep. We hear nothing, see nothing, and feel nothing but dryness, desolation, boredom, and tedium. But if we remain there humbly, patiently, and courageously, God secretly gives us every good gift, grace, and blessing. Such is the meaning of similar words we come across in another Psalm, "Although I am asleep, my heart continues to watch." Although our sense may seem asleep in prayer, we continue to wait and watch in a spirit of child-like faith and trust. This type of prayer is always richly rewarded and abundantly answered.

In order to receive the grace of prayer it is important that we free our hearts of all attachments and empty them of all desires. Attachments to creatures and desires for things other than God are the greatest obstacles to prayer.

Jesus says, "Blessed are the poor of heart, for theirs is the kingdom of God." A heart is poor when it is totally free of all attachments to created things. In another place in the Gospel, Jesus says, "You must renounce all that you possess in order that you may become My disciples." We must also renounce all that we possess if we wish to pray in the name of Jesus.

Jesus also says, "Blessed are the pure of heart, they shall see God." The object of prayer is to see God, to be one with Him, to be united with Him. But desires trouble the heart and darken the eyes of the soul. They prevent us from seeing God. Thus we must purify our heart of all desires, and desire God and Him alone. In this sense we read in the Psalms, "All my happiness lies in God alone." It is refreshing and spiritually delightful to come before the Lord to pray with a heart free of all attachments except the attachment to God, and a heart empty of all desires, except the desire for God and Him alone.

In the Old Testament, God spoke to the Prophet Hosea, "I will lead you into the desert, and there I shall speak to your heart." The desert is a symbol of the emptiness of all attachments and all desires. God speaking to the heart is the symbol of the union of the soul with God. The spiritual union takes place only in the total absence and emptiness of all attachments and desires. Again, in the Psalms, we read, "Be still and you shall know your God." The heart is still only if it is empty of all desires. Desires agitate the heart and they prevent it from knowing God and from resting in Him.

Again, in the Gospel, Jesus indirectly speaks of prayer when He tells the story of the poor widow. The poor widow in the story enters the temple, and puts in the offering box just two coins -- two "mites" -- which have very little monetary value. But these two coins represent the widow's life's savings. In a word, they are all that she has to give. Accordingly, Jesus praises her sacrifice and holds her up as a model.

We can apply this parable to the practice of prayer. When we come before God to pray, in a spiritual sense we are very much like the poor widow. We are not great intellectuals, nor do we have the great learning of theologians, nor the marvelous mystical powers of many of the saints. Conscious of our spiritual poverty, we humbly offer to God all that we have to give -- which are these two spiritual coins of good will and effort. These two coins represent all that we have to give. We can give no more. This prayer of goodwill and effort is a "perfect" prayer which is pleasing and acceptable to God, and which obtains an abundance of grace and blessing.

Goodwill means that when we come to pray, we seek God and God alone -- not our own selfish satisfaction, gratification, or consolation. We come before the Lord with a burning will and with a true desire to offer Him our mind and our heart. We seek Him and Him alone. We truly desire to pray, not just to waste time, show off, or indulge our laziness, and sleep as did the apostles in the Garden of Gethsemane.

This will to pray must be accompanied by a real and sincere effort. During prayer we truly try -- try our very best -- to rid our hearts of all distractions, to focus our attention, to concentrate our thoughts, to be alert, awake, and at all times to watch and wait upon the Lord. This type of prayer is perfect and holy, pleasing and acceptable to God, and marvelously fruitful and productive. Our feelings, emotions, impressions, and sentiments are of little or no importance. If each time we pray we offer these two coins -- our good will and our effort -- our prayer is truly a prayer in the name of Jesus; that is, according to his mind, heart, and spirit.

The prayer of the Sisters of Mary is centered on three devotions: 1) devotion to the Eucharist, 2) devotion to Mary, and 3) devotion to the Saints.

Our prayer of preference, of course, is the Mass and Communion. Adoration of the Eucharist is an extension of the eucharistic liturgy and a form of spiritual communion. Secondly, we love to pray to Mary. We especially love her prayer which is the rosary. We recite the rosary frequently and we try our best to recite it with joy, child-like fervor, love, and devotion. Thirdly, we love to pray to the saints. We love to read their lives and writings, to meditate upon them, to apply them to our daily lives, and to try our best to imitate them. The saints are the "words of God." God speaks to us through the saints.

Through them we learn more and more about Jesus, and are inspired to follow and imitate Jesus as the saints followed and imitated Him.

In conclusion, the Sister of Mary takes five vows. These are a reminder of the five wounds in the crucified body of Jesus.

The vow of poverty is a reminder of the wound in the right hand of Jesus. By poverty we nail to the cross our desire for material possessions.

The vow of chastity is a symbol of the wound in the left hand of Jesus. By this vow we nail to the cross the lust of the body and the satisfaction of the flesh.

The vow of obedience can be likened to the wound in the right foot of Jesus. From this vow, we nail to the cross our most precious possession which is our will.

The vow of service reminds us of the wound in the left foot of Jesus. By this vow we nail to the cross our time, energy, health, and strength.

Finally, the vow of prayer serves as a reminder of the wound in the side of Jesus. From this sacred wound in the side of Jesus flows a constant stream of blood and water which is a symbol of love and the light of faith.

Similarly, from our fifth vow of prayer flows the love of Jesus for the poor, and our faith in Jesus' presence in the poor.

"Pray always and never grow weary," says Jesus in the Gospel. By praying intensely everyday for about three hours, and lightly, easily, and in a child-like manner, all day and night, we will never grow weary of the consecrated life. Nor will we grow tired, bored, and "burned-out" in our daily life of poverty, chastity, obedience, and service. Each day, by being faithful to the vow of prayer and the spirit of prayer, we will be able to run lightly in the way of the Lord, and to run with joy and zest until we eventually complete the course and cross the finish line.

CHAPTER 12

PURSUIT OF PERFECTION

The call of Christ is a call to perfection.

On every page of the Gospels and Epistles, in one form or another, we come across this unrelenting call to perfection, holiness, and constant change. For example, in the Gospel Christ says, "As your Father in Heaven is perfect, so too must you become perfect." Again Jesus says, "As your Heavenly Father loves, so too must you love." In a similar vein St. Paul writes, "As God forgives us, so too must we forgive each other."

Again in the Gospel Jesus says, "As I have loved you, so too must you love each other." At the Last Supper Jesus looks at His disciples and says, "As you have seen Me do to you, so too must you do to each other."

God, Himself says, "As I am holy, so too must you become holy." And St. Paul writes, "It is the will of God to remake each one of us into the image and likeness of His only Son, Jesus Christ."

To be holy and perfect means to become like Jesus in every way. Jesus is the "new Adam," the perfect man, and the model of what I am to become. My goal is to become like Jesus in every way -- to think, speak, and act like Jesus. In essence, this is the meaning of holiness and perfection.

Since this is God's will for me, I too must be imbued with the same will. This will to be holy, perfect, and completely Christ-like is essential for growth and progress in the spiritual life.

God may be compared to a master sculptor who is infinitely skilled in his craft. Jesus is the model, and I am the clay. In order for God to shape, mold, and remake me into the image of this perfect model, who is Jesus, the clay with which He works must be soft, moist, and malleable. No matter how skilled the sculptor, if the clay is dry, hard, and brittle, the sculptor can do little with it. The clay would only break and crumble at his touch and fall to pieces in his hands.

I make the clay soft, moist, and malleable by imbuing it with a burning will to become holy and perfect like Jesus -- in a word, to become a saint. Then God, the master sculptor, can practice His craft with utmost ease. He can produce a beautiful, attractive, and glorious masterpiece which He delights in showing off to the saints and angels in Heaven.

One day the sister of St. Thomas Aquinas came to him with the question, "What must I do to become a saint?" He answered, "Will it! Will it!"

This real, driving, blazing will to become a saint should not be confused with mere wishful thinking. Thinking in a vague manner that perhaps it would be nice to become a saint, and that yes, one day I should try to become a saint is quite different from one who possesses this real, almost compulsive and obsessive will to become a saint. One with a real will to become a saint thinks about it day and night; adopts this as his life's goal, and pursues it with undeviating singleness of purpose. He says to himself, "Even if it should kill me, I will try my very best to become holy and perfect because this is the will of God for me."

In this sense, St. Augustine prayed, "Oh God, I am not perfect, but I wish to be perfect." St. Augustine also wrote, "What this one or that one has done (referring to the saints) so, too, can I." St. Ignatius of Loyola, lying on his sick bed recovering from his battle wounds, read the lives of the saints. Subsequently, there arose within him the driving ambition and the burning desire to become like them. St. Ignatius would say to himself, "What Dominic has done and what Francis has done, so too can I." This is what is meant by a real will to become a saint.

St. Therese of Lisieux had such a will from her earliest years. One night, while strolling with her father, she looked up at the configuration of the stars in the heavens and exclaimed, "Oh, Father, my name is already written in the heavens." She was referring to the letter "T" which she could make out in the configuration of the stars. Therese felt this call to holiness early and made it her personal goal in life. Moreover, she pursued this goal with that undeviating singleness of purpose which characterizes all men of God.

Shortly after entering the Carmel of Lisieux, Therese went to confession to a young priest, and revealed to him her personal ambition to become a saint -- even a great saint, such as St. Teresa of Avila. The priest was shocked by this revelation, scolded Therese for what he judged to be a movement of pride and girlish presumption. Therese held her ground and defended her position with the argument, "But, Father, does not Jesus tell us to become perfect, and can Jesus ask us to do something which is impossible?"

At the beginning of His public life, Jesus went from village to village, and synagogue to synagogue, relentlessly repeating the same message, which was essentially a call to holiness and perfection. He said, "Repent. Repent, for the Kingdom of God is at hand." In another place in the Gospel, Jesus in a similar manner said, "I have not come to call the just, but sinners -- and to bring them to repentance."

Here Jesus uses the word "just" in a somewhat sarcastic manner. Here the word "just" refers to those who have no spirit of repentance, such as the Pharisees. On the contrary, the Pharisees were filled with complacency, self-righteousness, and a sense of his moral superiority.

One who is truly contrite and repentant, in the sense that Jesus uses these words, is always filled with a certain holy dissatisfaction with self. He is always trying to change, to become different from what he now is, and each day to become more holy, perfect, and Christ-like.

In the Gospels, Jesus reserves His harshest words for those who do not have this dynamic will to change, to become different, and to become more and more holy and perfect. For example, Jesus says, "I would have you hot or cold, but lukewarm I will vomit you out of my mouth." There is a popular saying which goes, "Jesus loves you the way you are." This is false; Jesus loves you only if you are truly trying to become different from what you now are. There is another popular saying: "Accept yourself the way you are." In effect Jesus preaches the contrary: "You must constantly change, and try to become different from the way you now are."

Although St. John Vianney was already an old man of almost seventy, he was still filled with a holy dissatisfaction with self which gave him no rest. He looked upon himself as a great sinner, and longed to spend his final years in a Trappist Monastery praying, doing penance, and trying to become truly perfect and holy.

A true will to perfection will allow one no rest. In the religious life, one can never be complacent, morally relaxed, nor spiritually soft and lazy. St. Paul writes, "Forgetting what is behind, I always move forward and try to grasp what is ahead." Someone once asked St. John Vianney the question, "How must I go to Heaven?" He answered, "Like a cannonball." In other words, one must pursue this goal of holiness and perfection, which always lies beyond one's reach, with the forcefulness and directness of a ball shot from a cannon.

Christ's call to holiness is a call to heroism. Response to this call requires tremendous courage, great strength of character, fierce determination, remarkable patience, and extraordinary perseverance. Few indeed there are who are willing to respond to Christ's call and to pursue realistically this Gospel goal of perfection and holiness.

In the Gospel Jesus says, "The way to life is narrow, the door thereto is small; and few indeed there are who find it." The way to the fullness of life which is holiness and perfection is constant sacrifice, abnegation, and self-denial. Few there are who are willing to venture on this way or to dare to enter by this door. In a similar vein Jesus says, "Many are called but few are chosen." Jesus calls many -- in fact, all -- to sanctity but few are chosen; that is, few are willing to answer this call.

It is important to distinguish between a saint and one who is merely good, pious, and fervent. A saint is one who not only practices virtue, but practices it habitually, and in an extraordinary manner. Such practice is rare and demands heroism. But this indeed should be the goal of every religious.

The devil is the "father of lies". He is an expert at cunning and a master of deceit. Accordingly, the devil tries to convince us that the goal of sanctity is totally unrealistic for the normal person, that is, for you and me. We hear this sneering, mocking voice in the innermost part of our soul which says, "But no one can make a silk purse out of a sow's ear." In other words, this goal of sanctity is not for the likes of someone so weak, imperfect, and mediocre as myself.

But this is certainly not the spirit of Christ. In the Gospel Christ says, "Nothing is impossible to him who believes." One who believes, that is, who totally relies on the strength and power of God, can move mountains and tear up sycamore trees by their roots and throw them into the sea.

In the Gospels Jesus shows us convincingly that He can make a silk purse out of a sow's ear. At Cana, Jesus made wine out of water. At the Last Supper, Jesus took bread and wine and transformed them into His own flesh and blood. I must be convinced then that nothing is impossible with God, and that Jesus, the Son of God, can make someone as weak as me holy, perfect, and like Himself in every way.

In this sense St. Paul writes, "The power of Jesus in us can do infinitely more than we dream of or imagine." To think sanctity is unrealistic for me and perfection is beyond my grasp is to doubt the power of Jesus and to question the action of God's grace on my soul.

Here it may be well to ask the question, who is it who makes a saint? Is it God who makes a saint? Or is it I, myself, who makes the saint? The answer to both questions is yes. Yes, it is God and His grace. And yes, it is my good will and constant effort. These must go hand in hand in order to achieve the masterpiece of sanctity which is God's will for me and the goal of my existence.

St. Augustine wrote, "God created us without our consent, but He will not sanctify us unless we consent to it." In this sentence, St. Augustine eloquently expresses the marvelous balance between God's grace and man's cooperation which are necessary to achieve sanctity and perfection.

St. Paul writes, "We are not redeemed by works of the law, but only by faith in Christ." St. James balances this statement by saying, "Faith without works is dead." In the Gospel Jesus says, "Without Me you can do nothing." But the reverse of this statement is also true: without me, that is, without my burning will and courageous effort, Jesus can do nothing in me, with me, and through me.

If I truly believe in Jesus, I must therefore believe in the possibility of perfection and my vocation to holiness. I must be convinced that by God's help I can indeed become a saint.

This unrelenting pursuit of perfection should be dynamic, energetic, almost compulsive and obsessive. But at the same time it should be something joyful, light-hearted, and child-like.

In the Psalms we read the words, "Let us run lightly in the way of the Lord." The "way of the Lord" is the way of perfection. Two things are required to run in the manner of a world-class champion: 1) maximum effort and 2) total relaxation. If a runner goes all out but tenses up, he becomes tight, his stride shortens, his pace slackens, and he cannot hope to win the race. A first class runner must master the skill of combining maximum effort with total relaxation.

And this is the way we should try to run in the way of the Lord; that is, all out -- but at the same time lightly. The pursuit of holiness requires, so to speak, relaxed concentration, casual intensity, and maximum but light-hearted effort. Without this holy combination and happy balance we run the risk of emotional, psychological injury, and eventual spiritual burn-out.

It is also written in the Psalms, "The just man falls seven times a day." The "just man" is the man of God, the man who runs in the way of the Lord, and who pursues this goal of Christian perfection. But even the just man falls frequently. He habitually commits faults and imperfections by thought, word, and action. But these faults and imperfections are not willed; they are inadvertent and not reflected upon in advance. They are the result of habit and "primary movement." They spring from weakness rather than malice. As such they do not offend Jesus and do not constitute a real obstacle to the pursuit of holiness. One should accept these failures with calm, serenity, and humility. After each fall one should lightly get up, ask for forgiveness, and then go forward.

St. Paul writes, "If I must glory, I will glory in my weakness." Here, St. Paul expresses that joyful, humble, and calm acceptance of one's failures which one should have without in any way reducing one's effort in the pursuit of holiness and perfection. We should look at failure as an opportunity to lower oneself and to humble oneself before the Lord. Frequently God is more pleased with our humility than our "perfection."

If we could become perfect easily and quickly, as we would like, we would easily and quickly be tempted to pride. At times we like to dream of being as pure, holy, and perfect as the angels in heaven. But the angels in heaven used their purity, holiness, and perfection to exalt themselves. As a result of their great pride, they fell from the heights of heaven into the depths of Hell. It was said of the sisters of the convent of Port Royal, who followed the Jansenistic Creed, "They were pure as angels, but proud as devils." In a similar sense there is a certain spiritual wisdom in the lyrics of the popular song which go, "Oh Lord, it is hard to be humble when you are so perfect in every way."

St. Paul who had attained great mystical heights and penetrated the secrets of the third heaven was at the same time constantly filled with a sense of his weakness, inadequacy, and imperfection. "The things I wish to do," wrote St. Paul, "I do not do; and those I do not wish to do, I do. Who will deliver me from this body of death? Only the grace of Christ Jesus!" What Jesus wants of us, then, more than anything else is a real, driving will to be holy and a constant courageous effort to be perfect. All we have to do is offer Jesus this will and effort, and He and His grace will do the rest.

Here, it may be well to ask the question: why do I wish to be perfect? I wish to be perfect, first and foremost, to give glory to God and to please Jesus. I wish to be perfect also for the good of my neighbor -- because it is my faults and imperfections which are obstacles to charity and most offensive to my brother. But most of all

I wish to be perfect for my own good, for my own benefit, and my own happiness.

There is a maxim in philosophy which states, "Virtue is its own reward." It is because of my lack of virtue; that is, my habitual faults, failings, and imperfections that I most frequently lose my peace of heart and I experience sadness, disappointment, and frustration. Through the attainment of perfection and the practice of virtue there comes a great sense of inner joy, fulfillment, and spiritual gratification. This is the "abundant life" of which Jesus speaks in the Gospels and which He comes to give to His "sheep".

While the pursuit of perfection is first and foremost for my own good, at the same time it is also a marvelous expression of fraternal charity. Sanctity is contagious, dynamic, and "diffusive of self". Accordingly, if you want to become a saint, associate with saints, get a spiritual director who is a saint, and enter a religious community which as a group is dynamically pursuing the goal of sanctity.

If you are running with a group of people who are running all out, you are naturally inclined to pick up your own pace and to put out a maximum effort. We are all greatly influenced, directly and indirectly, by the example of those closest to us. If I am pursuing perfection and making a constant effort towards the attainment of holiness, this inevitably stirs up the will in those about me to engage in the same holy pursuit.

In studying the history of the saints, it is striking to see how frequently they arrive in clusters. For example, although the first Jesuits were only six or seven in number, among them are at least three of four canonized saints including -- Ignatius, Francis Xavier, and Peter Faber. This is not by accident. The personal inner fire in the heart of the individual creates a burning desire in the hearts of his companions, and they help each other in achieving this highest goal of holiness and perfection.

There is one final observation I wish to make on the subject of perfection. We really have no choice: we must achieve perfection. The only question is whether we achieve it in this life -- or in the next.

Perfection is the "wedding garment" of which we read in the Gospel, and with which we must be clothed if we are to be admitted to God's eternal banquet. God is perfect. If we are to dwell with Him for all eternity, to sit at His table, and enjoy His everlasting banquet, we must become pure, holy, and perfect as He is. If we fail to attain this goal in this life, we must be purified and perfected in the next life. And this is accomplished in that strange, murky, and mysterious region called "purgatory". It is so much more glorious, rewarding, and satisfying to achieve the goal of perfection in this life -- rather than wait until the next.

We can compare this to someone who runs a marathon race of forty-two kilometers but runs it in a lukewarm manner. When he crosses the finish line, there is no thundering applause from the onlookers, no pats on the back, nor congratulatory embraces. There is no gold medal, crown of glory, nor winner's banquet. Instead, the eternal judge waiting at the finish line puts his arm around your shoulders and says quietly, "My daughter, I asked for an all-out effort but you put out only sixty percent. You can do better than that. So before you take your rest, enjoy the runner's banquet, and receive the winner's medal, you must run another ten kilometers." What a terribly inglorious and disappointing finish that would be! But this is really what awaits those who run the way of the Lord in a manner which is mediocre, lukewarm, and half-hearted when they cross the finish line at death.

St. Paul at the end of his life writes, "I have fought the good fight. I have finished my course. I have kept the faith. Now I shall receive a crown of eternal glory." We, too, shall receive this crown of eternal glory. And we shall receive it immediately after death, if we run the way of the Lord everyday with maximum effort and light-hearted joy and gusto.

CHAPTER 13

CHRIST AND THE CROSS

The goal of the spiritual life is to imitate Christ, resemble Him in every way, to follow Him, and to walk the way He walked.

But who is Christ? What is He like? How does one follow Him? What is the way that He walked?

About seven hundred years before His coming, the Prophet Isaiah describes the Christ who is to come in terms of suffering and pain. In the words of Isaiah, the Messiah who is to come is the "suffering servant of Yahweh...a man of sorrows, acquainted with grief...in Him there is neither beauty nor comeliness. He is as one struck by God...He has the appearance of a leper.... One cannot look at Him without immediately turning away in horror and revulsion."

Other Prophets of the Old Testament spoke of the coming Messiah in similar terms of suffering and pain. For example, the Messiah is described as "one whose garments are stained purple as if He had just come from the wine press after trampling out the grapes." The garments of the Messiah are stained purple and colored red by His own blood.

In the Psalms, the Messiah is spoken of as "a worm and not a man" -- because His suffering has reduced Him to such a pitiful and powerless state. Also in the Old Testament the question is put on the lips of the Messiah, "Tell me, is there any suffering like unto my suffering?"

Jesus describes Himself and speaks of His mission in similarly stark terms. For example, He says: "Unless the grain of wheat falls to the ground and dies, it remains alone. But if it dies, it shall bear much fruit." And again He says, "If any man wishes to come after Me, he must deny himself and take up his cross daily and follow Me."

In another place in the Gospel, Jesus says, "Blessed are those who suffer (as I suffer), for they shall be consoled." To imitate Jesus, then, it is not enough to sacrifice and suffer now and then. It is not a sometime kind of thing, an Advent or Lent type of penance. On the contrary, if one wishes to resemble Jesus and to be remade into His image and likeness, one must suffer daily, develop the habit of sacrifice, and constantly choose what is uncomfortable rather than what is comfortable.

As the Prophet Elias ascended into the heavens on a fiery chariot, his cloak fell on the shoulders of his disciple, Eliseus, who was called to follow after and to imitate him. In a similar manner, after Jesus ascended into the heavens, the cloak of the "suffering servant of Yahweh" fell on the shoulders of Paul of Tarsus. Like Jesus, Paul's life was one of continuing suffering, daily dying, and constant humiliation. When Jesus spoke of Paul to the church leader, Ananias, in Damascus, He said, "He is to be a vessel of election... I will show him how much he must suffer for My name."

The mystery of the cross became the central core of the thinking and theology of St. Paul. St. Paul became almost obsessed by the depth, the height, the beauty, and the grandeur of this fundamental mystery of suffering. St. Paul speaks of it constantly. For example, in his Epistle to the Corinthians he writes, "While I was among you, I knew only Christ and Christ crucified." He writes of this mystery on nearly every page of his Epistles. What is more, he writes not in a theoritical manner but from the depths of a daily, personal experience.

As has already been touched upon in the previous chapter, originally the cross of Christ was for St. Paul a scandal and a stumbling block. At the school of theology in Jerusalem which St. Paul attended, he had been taught by the rabbis that the cross was a sign of God's disfavor. Suffering was considered a punishment, and pain was a curse. Thus, Paul looked at Jesus nailed to the cross and was convinced that He was a fake and a blasphemer. If Jesus were truly the Messiah and the Son of God as He claimed to be, how could God possibly permit Him to suffer such pain, defeat, humiliation, and death? Convinced of the rightness of His position, Paul

in good faith hunted down the disciples of Christ, had
them arrested, jailed, tortured, and killed.

On the road to Damascus, in the light of the risen
Christ, Paul understood that his position was wrong and
that he was completely mistaken. He did a complete
turn-around and about face in his thinking. Now Paul
understood that the cross was a sign of God's favor, that
suffering was a gift, and that pain and humiliation were
graces from above. "God chastises him whom He loves."
"As gold and silver are purified by fire, so is the soul of
man made clean in the crucible of humiliation." These
and other similar words from the Old Testament were
familiar to Paul, but now in a flash, he grasped their
meaning; and he was filled with wonder and a sense of
personal discovery.

For Paul, the cross was no longer something to be
scorned, rejected, and to be fled from. On the contrary,
the cross was something precious to be sought after,
embraced, and valued.

As Jesus before him, Paul lived a life of constant and
intense suffering, pain, humiliation, worry, anxiety,
fear; and finally he suffered martyrdom and death.
Paul writes, "With Christ, I am nailed to the cross. It is
no longer I who live but Christ who lives in me." Again,
"I bear in my own body the marks of the passion of
Christ." In another place he writes, "Far be it from me
to glory in anything but the cross of Christ Jesus."
Again he writes, "All the day long I am put to death."
And, "I die daily." Again St. Paul writes, "If I must
glory, I will glory in my weakness." Here the word
"weakness" refers to the daily cross which Paul was
called upon to carry.

To follow Jesus means the cross. And the cross
means suffering, pain, humiliation, and death. It is not
something romantic, sentimental, nor philosophical.
Suffering is not a game. Pain is not child's play. And
death is no laughing matter. Human nature
instinctively recoils from the slightest pain, turns away
from the smallest discomfort, and flees from all
humiliation and whatever is unpleasant. Thus, to
follow Christ on the road to sanctity requires great
patience, heroic courage, extraordinary determination,

and outstanding perseverance. Christ calls all His disciples to sanctity by following this way of the cross. It is hardly surprising that He has so few followers.

In the Gospel Christ says, "Many are called but few are chosen." Many -- in fact, all -- are called to follow Christ on this way of the cross, but very few respond to this invitation, because of their fear and cowardice. Again Christ says, "The way to life is narrow and the door is small, and few there are who find it." The way and the door to this new life in God which is holiness and perfection is narrow and small. It is the way of the cross and the door to pain and death. Few indeed there are who find it.

St. John of the Cross refers to this understandable situation in his writings where he poses the question, "Why is it that there are so few truly holy souls among the disciples and believers of Jesus?" He answers his own question by the one word, "Cowardice". He goes on to explain that many enthusiastically begin to follow Christ but inevitably they encounter the cross. They easily lose heart, cowardly give up, and quickly turn back.

St. John of the Cross in his writings emphasizes again and again the absolute necessity to believe in and to love the cross if one wishes to resemble Christ. He writes, "It is absolutely essential to understand that you must plumb the depths of suffering and experience every pain if you wish to obtain the fullness of holiness in God. In fact, you must learn to love suffering and to put your joy in pain if you wish to attain the perfection to which Jesus summons you."

St. John did not simply write of the mystery of the cross in a speculative manner. He lived this mystery, experienced it daily, and plumbed its depths as few sons of Adam have been called upon to do. Humanly speaking, the suffering which St. John of the Cross was called upon to endure in his body and soul, was terrifying. St. John of the Cross always practiced perfect patience, heroic courage, outstanding determination, and continuing perseverance which are characteristics of all the Saints.

One day, while St. John of the Cross was praying before a crucifix in the chapel, Jesus spoke to him tenderly. Jesus said, "My son, you have done much for My glory. What do you desire as a reward?" The answer from the lips of St. John was, "Suffering and contempt." In the light of faith and from his own personal experience, St. John of the Cross looked upon suffering and contempt as gifts, graces, and blessings from God. He looked upon them as things to be desired and treasures in which are found the fullness of holiness and perfection.

St. Therese of Lisieux, as well as St. John of the Cross, her mentor, writes frequently of suffering. She does this not in a psychotic, and morbid manner, but with the same spirit of Christ which is always positive, triumphant, and optimistic.

Her first holy communion at the age of twelve was a peak experience of grace in her life. She writes that after this experience she felt arising from the depths of her heart a strong desire to suffer. She was amazed at this attraction for suffering and realized that such an attraction -- so contrary to human nature and instinct -- could come only from Jesus with whom she had been united in the Eucharist.

St. Therese writes, "Holiness is suffering". Holiness is not beautiful words, the shedding of warm tears, nor romantic feelings. It is suffering in every way, every day.

St. Therese is called the "Little Flower". In fact, because of her remarkable courage in the midst of every trial and suffering, St. Therese more closely resembles a mighty oak tree than a frail little flower. Therese entered Carmel at the age of 15 and she died at the age of 24. Her eight years of religious life were years of daily martyrdom and crucifixion. She suffered from constant inner dryness, spiritual emptiness, and boredom which were extremely hard to bear for one called to a life of daily prayer for six or seven hours. She suffered from the physical hardship of life in Carmel which included disagreeable food, lack of sleep and rest, and the terrible, killing cold and dampness. She suffered frequent sore throats, indigestion, sleepless nights, and constant fatigue. She suffered the misunderstanding of her superiors and their constant inadvertent humiliation of a soul tender and sensitive. Her father's mental illness was put on her account. After Therese entered Carmel, the shock of losing his "little queen" caused her father to lose his reason, and for three years he was mentally ill. At one point he even threatened to kill his own daughters with a pistol. For Therese, this was a horrible humiliation, and a source of inner conflict and torment.

The final two or three years of her life were years of terrible sickness. She came down with tuberculosis, not just pulmonary tuberculosis, but tuberculosis of the intestines. The physical pain was so horrible that at one point she was even tempted to suicide. And then her final year or two of life was marked by a mysterious temptation against faith which caused her much inner tension, turmoil, and agony. Yet Therese hid her suffering behind a smile, and endured it with remarkable courage and that heroic patience, determination, and perseverance which characterizes the saints of God.

In the Book of the Revelations, St. John the apostle had a vision of the saints in glory. In the course of this revelation, the question is asked, "Who are they who are clothed in these white garments?" And the answer from heaven is, "These are they who have come from the great tribulation. They have washed their robes white in the blood of the lamb." The "blood of the lamb" is the blood of Jesus. It is a symbol of suffering. To become white, pure, and holy in the sight of God, then, one must wash his robes daily in the blood of Jesus -- which is suffering, sacrifice, humiliation, and death.

At times we have a mistaken notion of the suffering of Jesus. We say it was horrible enough, but after all it only lasted three hours. Or if we calculate the time from the moment of Jesus' arrest to the moment of his demise, maybe only fifteen hours. But there is a hidden, mysterious, unlimited quality to the suffering of Jesus. In terms of time, His suffering may have been only of short duration; but in a sense it was unlimited in its intensity, pain, and horror, because it was the suffering of the God-Man. In the Old Testament, the question is put on the lips of the Messiah, "Tell me is there any suffering like unto mine?" The answer to this question is "no". There is really no suffering like unto that of Jesus. His suffering is unique and horrifying to a degree which we will only understand in the vision of glory.

In the Apostles' Creed, in reference to Jesus, we recite these strange words, "He descended into hell." St. Thomas Aquinas interprets these words as meaning that Jesus descended to the depths of all human suffering, that He tasted all pain, and drank the cup of humiliation to the dregs. Jesus experienced in His body and soul all the pain, suffering, and humiliation which man is capable of.

In this sense, St. Paul writes, "In all things except sin, Jesus was like unto us, and He experienced suffering like unto us, so that in our suffering He might console us." In our suffering and pain, no matter how intense, we cannot look at Jesus and say, "Lord, I know you sympathize with me, but really, you do not understand. You do not know what it is like." Jesus does know what it is like because He has been there Himself. He has experienced it, before me in His flesh and in His soul.

In the cross there is always an element of fear. Jesus Himself experienced this fear, horror, and terror when He was faced with the cross. This reaction on His part is most consoling to us. In the Garden of Gethsemane, Jesus trembles, falls to the ground, presses His face to the earth, and sweats blood. He cries out, "My soul is sorrowful even unto death." He was depressed, even to the point of death at the thought of the cross. Even after consenting to the cross, in the darkness of Calvary, Jesus cried out, "My God, My God, why have you abandoned me?" Through these words He expresses the terrible feeling of darkness and despair which had grasped and gripped His heart. If we too did not experience fear in the face of the cross, it would not be for real; and we would not truly be creatures of flesh and blood.

St. Paul in his writings speaks of the strange trial at Ephesus in which he fought with the beasts, and was so discouraged and depressed that he wanted to give up and die. St. Therese was also, as mentioned before, tempted to suicide in her intense pain. In the Old Testament, the Prophet Elias had all he could take of trial and tribulation, and wanted nothing more than to lay down and die.

At times, we like to think of suffering in romantic terms. We imagine ourselves as the hero enduring the worst which life has to offer with bright eyes and a smiling countenance. We secretly imagine the scene. We are surrounded by friends and acquaintances on our bed of pain. They look at us lying there with an angelic smile and heroic patience. And they exclaim, "Ooh and aah, look at the beautiful saint!" Inwardly, we repeat the same exclamation, and say to ourselves, "Ooh and aah, look at my remarkable heroism and beautiful courage!"

The point is that even in intense suffering there is always an inherent temptation to pride and self-exaltation. Accordingly, in our suffering and pain God permits us to taste our weakness, experience our impatience, and feel our lack of courage -- as a constant reminder that we are made only of dust and clay. In this way, suffering is always positive in its fruits and does not subtly lead us into feelings of self-satisfaction and pride. St. Paul writes, "God is faithful. He never permits us to be tried beyond our strength. With each trial He gives us the strength to endure it." St. Paul, buffeted by an "angel of Satan," experienced great pain and cried out to the Lord three times for pity and deliverance. The Lord answered, "My grace is sufficient for you." Like St. Paul, we too in our suffering cry out for deliverance. Jesus hears our cry and speaks to our hearts the same words He spoke to Paul: "My grace is sufficient for you."

Suffering is the supreme test of faith, confidence, and trust in God. The problem is that we would like very much for the grace and strength of Jesus to be more than sufficient; but it is enough and just enough for that suffering, for that trial, and for that moment.

Again St. Paul writes,"I can do all things in Him who strengthens me." Similarly, St. Paul in another place writes, "In all of these difficulties I can more than overcome in Him who loves me."

The secret to enduring the cross of Jesus is to trust in
His strength, and be convinced that it is enough, and
that it will be given to us from moment to moment,
instant to instant -- as needed. We should not worry
about the future, nor should we ask ourselves how we
can endure this or that trial or tribulation for a year, for
a day, for an hour, or even for a minute. We must focus
on the present instant, and learn to live from instant to
instant trusting totally in the power of Jesus and relying
completely on the strength of God.

In God, there is no time, no past, nor future. All is
now -- an eternal, ever-renewed now. If we are in God
by faith and love, we develop the habit of living in the
present instant and entrusting the future to His
providence. It is in this spirit, that Jesus in the Gospel
says, "Do not be concerned about tomorrow -- enough for
the day is the evil thereof."

One saint wrote, "Suffering is in me, but I am not in
it. I am in God." We are in God by faith, hope and love.
In suffering and pain we should try our best at all times
to turn away from self, to entrust ourselves to God, and
to keep our gaze fixed only on Him. Whatever we fix our
attention on automatically grows in importance and
gathers weight. Thus, we should try to focus our
attention not on the pain, suffering, and difficulty in our
lives, but to turn away from them and looking only at
Jesus, beg for His strength. And Jesus will give us
enough patience, courage, and strength for that
moment, and that moment alone.

St. John the apostle in his First Epistle writes, "Love
casts out fear. Where there is perfect love, there is no
fear." In other words, if your heart is filled with love
there is no room for the negative emotions of fear,
anxiety, sadness, depression, or self-pity. The secret,
then, to handling suffering and pain is found in love
which takes us out and away from self and fixes our
attention on the object of our affection.

Jesus in His agony gives us an example of the power
of love to overcome suffering. His heart was troubled
even unto death; but His attention was constantly
focused on others. At the Last Supper, He forgot His
own inner torment and tried to console His disciples. He

said, "Let not your hearts be fearful, or your minds be troubled." And again He said, "My peace I give you, My peace I leave with you." After His arrest in the Garden of Gethsemane, Jesus' immediate thought was for the welfare of His disciples. "If you seek Me," He said, "let these others go." On the way to Calvary, Jesus looked at the women weeping and wailing for Him and consoled them with the words, "Weep not for Me, but for yourselves and for your children." Although in intense pain on the cross, Jesus thought of His mother and the disciple, John, whom He loved; and He spoke words of comfort and consolation to them. He looked at the Good Thief and spoke words of hope to him. And finally, Jesus looked at His enemies who surrounded Him, pleaded their cause before His Father in heaven, and begged for forgiveness.

On Calvary, Jesus also prayed, "My God, my God, why have you forsaken Me?" And again, "My God, into thy hands I commend My spirit." Throughout His suffering, Jesus was not absorbed by self, nor preoccupied with His own pain and suffering. He breaks out of the prison of self-consciousness, self-centeredness, and self-pity, and constantly renews acts of love. Jesus constantly looks at God and speaks to Him; or else He looks at others and thinks primarily of their good and their welfare. This is what we must try to do in our suffering. Lightly and easily, but always with courage and determination, we must look away from self, fix our gaze in God, or else we look at others and in imitation of Jesus are concerned only with their welfare and good. In this constant practice of love we overcome suffering, conquer pain, and endure every difficulty in the manner which Jesus teaches us.

In the Gospel Jesus says, "In the world you shall have tribulation, but take courage, I have overcome the world." We, too, overcome the world and its trials and tribulations by imitating Jesus in the practice of courageous, and unselfish love.

Not only love, but hope also is a source of patience and strength in suffering and difficulty. St. Paul writes, "Hope engenders patience." In the light of hope we see through the darkness of suffering and discover the radiant light of glory which is its reward. In the

Gospels, Jesus always speaks of His suffering in terms of hope, victory, and glory. For example, He says, "The time for the glorification of the Son of Man is at hand." And after His resurrection, Jesus says, "Did not the Son of Man have to suffer all of these things in order to enter into His glory?" In the light of hope we look at suffering and see that it is simply a measure of our future glory. In the light of hope we see suffering and realize that it is something passing and temporary which leads to eternal joy and happiness. In this spirit Jesus says, "You will fall into sadness and weep and wail, but your sadness will be turned into joy. And no one can take this joy from you."

St. Paul always writes of the mystery of the cross in terms of glory and looks at suffering in the light of hope. For example, St. Paul says, "I consider the sufferings of the present moment as nothing when compared to the future glory which will be ours." And again, he says, "Our light, passing, and temporary affliction will earn for us a weight of eternal glory."

St. Stephen, the first martyr, is an example of that radiant hope which fills the heart of the Christian and from which flows the divine patience needed to endure the worst sorrow and suffering. The enemies of Christ rushed at Stephen, dragged him from the city, and began stoning him to death. But in the Acts of the Apostles, it is written that "his face shone like an angel". St. Stephen looked above and saw the heavens open, and gazed upon the risen, glorified Christ. He looked above and saw the glory which awaited him if he endured this suffering, violence, and death in the name of Jesus. This courage, patience, and perseverance came from his total trust in the promise of Jesus. Another name for this unshakable trust in the promise of Jesus is "hope".

Hope in our heart tells us that the sufferings of this present life are for a moment and that they lead to eternal glory and happiness. If we look to the heavens in the light of hope, we too can see through the clouds and gaze at the glory which awaits us.

Another element found in the cross of Christ is a new, secret, spiritual joy. In the Gospel Jesus says,

"Blessed are they who suffer." There is, then, a certain blessedness or happiness in suffering which begins now in this world and attains its fullness later in the next world. It is in this sense that St. Paul writes, "I know how to rejoice in all my tribulations." Again, St. Paul writes, "God consoles us in all our afflictions." And still again, in a similar sense, St. Paul says, "Although the passion of Christ abounds in me, His glory and comfort do super-abound."

There is no contradiction here. On the surface, there can be intense pain, suffering, depression, and even feelings of despair. But underneath, in the depths of the heart, there flows a cool, pure, secret stream of peace and joy which has its source in God. In the words of the psalmist, "God knows that we are made only of dust and clay." In other words, God knows how weak, fragile, and cowardly we are. In order to encourage us in suffering and tribulation, God gives us this inner quiet, secret joy which acts, in a sense, as a spiritual sedative or pain killer, and gives us the courage to go forward and the patience to endure unto the end.

St. Thomas Aquinas has written, "Man cannot live without happiness." So it is that God in our suffering gives each of us that measure of happiness necessary to keep us going. God always gives us "breathing space". Even in intense suffering, He gives us the opportunity to catch our breath, to get a second "spiritual wind," to be refreshed, and to go on.

After St. Peter stated that he had renounced all for the sake of Jesus, he asked what reward could he expect in return. Jesus answered by promising three rewards: 1) the cross, 2) eternal glory and happiness, and 3) hundredfold more happiness in this life. In the cross then there is an abundant measure of spiritual joy, peace, happiness -- already in this world.

St. Paul writes, "In all circumstances, whether I am rich or poor, in abundance or need, whether I am hungry or satiated, I know how to be satisfied." In other words, St. Paul knows how to be satisfied, at peace, even happy among his daily trials, tribulations, and crosses. St. Therese of Lisieux speaks of her life in Carmel in terms of constant suffering, sacrifice, and hardship; but at the same time she constantly refers to this secret inner peace -- cool and refreshing as a gentle breeze -- which never leaves her. This phenomenon is something which only those who truly believe in and love the cross can grasp and understand.

In one poignant scene from the Gospels, Jesus turns to James and John and asks, "Can you drink of my chalice? Can you be baptized with my baptism? They answer, "Yes, we can." Indeed they were baptized with a baptism of fire, and they drank the chalice of pain and suffering to the dregs -- as Jesus, their Lord and Master.

In the silence of our hearts, Jesus asks us the same question, "Can you drink of my chalice?" We answer, "Yes, Lord, I can. I cannot by any strength of my own, but I can by your strength, power, courage, and patience."

St. Paul sums up the essence of the mystery of the Cross when he writes, "In the cross is salvation, life, and resurrection." In the cross of Christ is holiness; and outside of the cross, there is no holiness. It is as simple as that. If we are serious about sanctity and truly wish to pursue perfection, we must believe in the cross, and love the cross, and have the courage to carry it everyday in union with Jesus.

CHAPTER 14

LET US SERVE THE LORD WITH JOY

"Let us serve the Lord with joy." These words from the Psalms are the motto of the Sisters of Mary.

St. Francis of Assisi once said, "The devil loves a sad heart." St. Paul writes contrary-wise, "God loves a cheerful giver."

Our God is a God of peace and joy. We should serve Him always with peace and joy. What is more, we should exteriorize the peace and joy in our hearts by a smile on our lips, spiritual laughter on our faces, and the light of Christ in our eyes. It has been said of St. Francis Xavier that although he never seemed to laugh, there was always laughter on his face. Men will be attracted to Christ and give glory to God by the spiritual peace and joy radiating from our person.

It has been said that in the Bible one can count 365 instances -- one for each day of the year -- in which we are admonished, "Do not be troubled. Do not be afraid. Do not be anxious." The point is that always, everyday, and all day, we should try to serve the Lord with lighthearted trust, child-like joy, and cheerful abandonment.

St. Paul was in prison in Rome, chained day and night to his jailer, not knowing from one day to the next when he would be dragged out to have his head separated from his body. Yet St. Paul writes to the Christians at Philippi, "Rejoice. Again I say to you, rejoice always in the Lord." The joy we are to practice then is not based on fair weather, sound sleep, and good digestion. It is based on the Lord. It is a supernatural joy, which we are called upon to practice at all times and in all circumstances.

In another one of his letters, St. Paul writes, "In all circumstances, whether I am in need or whether I have abundance, whether I am rich or poor, whether I am hungry or satiated, I know how to be satisfied." St. Paul is stating that in all circumstances, no matter what happens, the follower of Christ never loses the peace and joy in his heart. What is more, he must constantly give witness to this peace and joy. There radiates from his person a certain attractive spiritual calm, serenity, and happiness.

For example, in the Gospel we see Jesus standing before a multitude of people who are desperately poor, downtrodden, and suffering in so many ways. Jesus says to them, "Come to me all you who labor and are heavily burdened. I will refresh you. You will find peace for your souls. My burden is light, my yoke is sweet." It is difficult to imagine a sad, irritated, depressed, frowning, or angry Jesus speaking such words. His enemies would have ridiculed Him and laughed Him to scorn. On the contrary, we can easily imagine a joyful, serene, even smiling Jesus speaking these words. Men were naturally attracted to the person of this Jesus who was "meek and humble of heart." And from all sides, the poor, the downtrodden, and the little ones came to Him to be healed, consoled, and enlightened.

In another place in the Gospel, Jesus says concerning the children of the poor, "Suffer the little ones to come unto me and prevent them not, for of such is the kingdom of heaven." After saying this, Jesus takes the children into His arms one by one, caresses and blesses them. Children are normally repelled by someone who is sad, angry, scowling, frowning, or depressed. But they were not repelled by Jesus; on the contrary, they were attracted to Him, and went to Him with complete trust and abandonment.

And still in another place in the Gospel Jesus says, "Blessed are they who work for peace, they shall be called the sons of God." Jesus Himself "worked for peace," and constantly gave witness to this peace of God by His words, attitude, and actions. What is more, He generously shared His peace with those about Him.

Mary, the mother of Jesus, is a model of one who serves the Lord with peace and joy. After her total surrender to God at the time of the annunciation, Mary runs with lighthearted joy to her cousin, Elizabeth. When Mary and Elizabeth meet, the babe in the womb of her cousin leaps for joy. Mary is a "living tabernacle". Jesus, the source of all joy, dwells in her heart by faith and love, and in her body, by the power of the Holy Spirit. As Jesus, Mary too, constantly gives witness to the peace and joy of God in her heart, and generously shares it with those with whom she comes into contact. After exchanging greetings with Elizabeth, Mary sings the Magnificat -- a lighthearted hymn of praise and thanksgiving to God who is the source of true peace and joy.

At the wedding feast of Cana, Mary again gives witness indirectly to the joy and peace of the Lord. She is the "mystical rose," inclined by temperament to silence, solitude, and contemplation. But she goes to Cana to participate in the wedding feast in order to increase the innocent joy and happiness of her friends.

At the time of Jesus, wedding feasts sometimes lasted for two or three days. An abundance of good wine was essential for a successful fiesta, but at Cana the wine gave out. It is Mary who notices this lack, calls the attention of Jesus to it, and then entrusts the matter to Him.

Wine gives joy to the heart, strength to the body, causes people to laugh, sing, dance, and rejoice. As such, it is a symbol of joy. After the wine had given out at Cana, Jesus makes wine out of water -- due primarily to the initiative of Mary. Not only does Jesus make wine, but He makes an abundance of the best tasting wine. Here we see that Mary, through the power of Jesus, gives joy to the children of men, increases their happiness, and creates an atmosphere which is warm, bright, and cheerful.

When Mary appears to the children of men in visions, there usually radiates from her person a very attractive, bright, youthful, and dynamic peace and joy. For example, Mary appears to the poor Indian peasant, Juan Diego in 1531 at Guadalupe, Mexico, as a beautiful, radiant, youthful Indian princess. Mary speaks to Juan Diego most tenderly in words reminiscent of those used by Jesus in the Gospel. Mary says, "My loving son, my little Juan Diego, why are you troubled? Am I not here? Am I not your mother? Are you not in my heart? Will anything be lacking to you?"

Again at Banneux, Belgium, in 1933, Mary appears to the 12 year old child, Mariette Beco, as the smiling "Virgin of the poor." Mary's garments are white, and there is a fullness of light which surrounds her and radiates from her person. In many ways, Mary resembles the transfigured Jesus of Mount Thabor. The poor, rustic Mariette Beco is greatly attracted, both by the love of Mary, and also by this youthful, radiant, spiritual peace and joy.

The peace and joy which we strive to practice, to give witness to, and to share with those about us is above all a spiritual and supernatural peace and joy. As already touched upon in the previous chapter, this peace and joy is based upon and flows from the theological virtues of faith, hope, and charity.

St. John the apostle has written, "Where there is love, there is no fear. Perfect love casts out all fear." Love, then, is the antidote to "fear," which is a symbol of all negative emotions -- such as sadness, depression, anxiety, despondency, and guilt.

As mentioned previously, although there is really only one charity or love, it can be expressed in three ways. First of all, there is love of God which is expressed by prayer; then we have love of neighbor, which is called brotherly love; and finally there is love of the poor, which is expressed by service. If we practice love in these three ways, our hearts will be filled with the peace and joy of Christ.

In the Gospel, we are somehow consoled to see how Jesus expresses the feelings in His heart, and does not hide them from His friends. For example, on at least two occasions in the Gospel, Jesus weeps, because it is only natural for a man to weep when His heart is saddened. On another occasion Jesus expresses the irritation and impatience He feels in His heart. Jesus says, "How long must I be with you? How long must I endure you? Along the same line, Jesus expresses the terrible torment and anguish He feels in His heart at the thought of His approaching passion and death. Jesus says, "My heart is troubled. And what shall I say? Oh Father, deliver Me from this hour." In the Garden of Gethsemane, the heart of Jesus is sorrowful even unto death, His body trembles with terror, and with His face pressed to the earth, He sweats blood. Then He prays, "Father, if possible let this chalice pass from me." Finally, on the cross of Calvary enveloped by darkness, Jesus expresses the feelings of despair and despondency in His heart when He cries out, "My God, my God, why have you abandoned Me?" And again, He expresses His bodily pain by the words, "I thirst."

The Psalms are the prayers of the Holy Spirit. Fully one-third of them are an expression of human suffering and a cry for help to God. Under the impulse of the Holy Spirit, the psalmist cries out in anguish, he sighs, he groans, he points to the terrible suffering, the danger, the fear, and the humiliation in his life. We learn from this that it is proper and even pleasing to God for us to express our pain, fear, anxiety, and sadness. We are permitted to sigh, groan, and even to cry out in our pain. We do this before our friends. And we do this before God. But, we do it lightly and easily -- in order to ease the pain, release the pressure, and lighten the load. But quickly, we turn our gaze from the suffering itself, and look at God with faith and love. Then, we remain with our gaze fixed on the beauty of the face of God in contemplation, and lose ourselves in God through prayer. In this way, we can say, "Although suffering is in me, I am not in it. I am in God." In this way, we learn too how to "suffer without suffering."

This is the way Jesus conducted Himself during His pain and suffering. He constantly looks away from these feelings, and looks at God in a continuing act of contemplation. For example, in the garden He prays again and again, "Father, thy will be done." On the cross, He cries out, "My God, my God, why have You forsaken Me?" And again, "My God, into Thy hands I commend My Spirit."

In the garden, Jesus goes to His friends for consolation. He tells them to watch with Him -- in a word, to share His anguish and pain. But His closest friends, Peter, James, and John, only disappoint Him, and make His suffering worse. We too are permitted to seek comfort, consolation, and support from our friends; but, more often than not, we will end up by being disappointed. In the garden of Gethsemane, Jesus turns to God, and God sends an angel who comes to comfort Him. St. Paul writes, "Our lives are buried with Christ in God." In the spirit of these words, in all pain, anguish, and suffering we go through Christ to the Father, and we lose ourselves in Him through prayer and contemplation.

St. John the apostle has also written, "Whoever loves his brother is in God, and God is in him." Brotherly love is another antidote to sadness, anxiety, and all negative emotions. If we love our brother we are in God who is infinite joy and peace. Through the practice of brotherly love, we are in God's joy and peace, and they are in us.

Jesus Himself in the Gospel refers to this when He says, "Blessed are they who show mercy, they shall receive mercy." Blessed are those who love, they shall receive love and with it, the peace and joy of God.

In order to love one's neighbor or brother, one must hate himself. To think of one's brother, one must forget himself. To go to someone in order to help him, one must leave self, be indifferent to self, get out of self, abandon, and renounce self.

By nature, we are so inclined to selfishness. By instinct, we are so preoccupied with self, absorbed by self. We are excessively self-centered and self-conscious. These inclinations rob our hearts of peace, joy, and inner happiness. If you were to visit a mental hospital, you would be impressed to see how self-conscious and self-absorbed the mentally ill are. Try as they will, they simply cannot get out of themselves, away from self, and think of others. In a word, they are incapable of loving.

The healthiest personality is that of one who is the least concerned with self -- the one who loves. If we forget self, think only of Jesus in our neighbor, and seek always to please Jesus in our brother, we, at the same time, cast out fear and overcome all the negative emotions embedded in our hearts.

Finally, love and service of the poor are antidotes to fears and negative emotions. In the parable of the Good Samaritan, Jesus in effect says, "If you wish to find life -- that is, true peace and joy -- you must do as this Samaritan." The Samaritan abandoned his own plans, renounced his own interest, went to the poor man set upon by robbers, and served him as his own flesh and blood. Jesus concludes the story by saying, "You, too, go and do likewise. And you shall live." If you give of yourself and serve the poor, as the good Samaritan, you will find this living joy and peace which Jesus comes to give.

Spiritual peace and joy has its source not only in love, but in faith also. In the Gospel, Jesus says, "Whoever believes in Me, there will spring up from within a river of living water." If you truly believe in Jesus there will spring up from the depths of your heart a never-ending stream of living joy.

First of all, by faith we believe that whatever God sends to us is sent out of love, and is sent for our own ultimate good. It is not important whether we understand the reason for the trials and tribulations which God sends to us. But by faith we trust in His love, and we have total confidence in His mercy.

Again, by faith, we know that whatever difficulty or pain God sends to us, at the same time, He sends us the strength, patience, and courage to endure them.

Again, faith teaches us that in every cross there is a secret spiritual joy and a hidden supernatural peace which more than compensate for the pain and suffering. Jesus expresses this mystery in the Gospel when He says, "Blessed are you who weep, for you shall be consoled."

Also, by faith, we trust completely in the forgiveness, mercy, and compassion of Jesus. Frequently, our hearts are heavy, and we are sometimes depressed because of a free-floating guilt, a sense of sin, and a vague feeling of shame caused by the memory of past sins or failures. This is offensive to God because it indicates that we do not truly trust in His mercy, compassion, and forgiveness.

Mary Magdalene was a sinful woman; in fact, Jesus cast seven demons out of her. Yet, after Jesus forgave her, she at the same time forgave herself and entirely entrusted her past to the mercy of Jesus. This childlike, lighthearted trust in the mercy of Jesus made her most pleasing to Him. In fact, in the Gospel, she becomes Jesus' closest friend. And at the same time, she becomes an exemplar of the trust and confidence which Jesus desires of us.

Another beautiful example of this trust and confidence can be found in the Good Thief on Calvary. He had lived an evil life, but all He did was look at Jesus and say, "Lord, remember me when you come into your kingdom." And Jesus answered, "This very day, you shall be with Me in paradise." Just a word, a gesture, a movement of sorrow and contrition is all that is necessary to obtain the mercy and forgiveness of Jesus.

Another lesson in compassion is found in the parable of the prodigal son. The son had not yet asked for forgiveness; but the father took the initiative, and ran to him, embraced him, and magnanimously forgave him. He gave the errant son new clothes, a ring for his finger; then he killed the fattened calf, and ordered a fiesta of forgiveness and thanksgiving. We must trust in God's forgiveness and mercy. As God forgives us, we must also forgive ourselves. What is more, after obtaining forgiveness, we should never look back. Rather we should forget our past mistakes and go forward with peace and joy.

Our joy and peace are also based on the theological virtue of hope. Hope in turn is based on absolute trust in the promise of Jesus about future reward. In the light of hope we are convinced that the sufferings of this life are simply a measure of future glory and happiness.

A beautiful example of serving the Lord with joy based on faith, hope, and charity can be found in the person of St. Therese of Lisieux. St. Therese's life in Carmel was one of daily martyrdom, yet she always hid her suffering behind a beautiful and radiant smile. It has been written, "If you have a thorn in your side and can still smile, then you are indeed a hero." St. Therese was such a hero.

Her peace, joy, and heroic cheerfulness in all circumstances reflect very much the teachings of Christ. In the Gospel, Christ admonishes His disciples, "When you fast, do not do as the hypocrites who disfigure their faces and appear gloomy before men, in order to win their praise. But when you fast, anoint your head and wash your face...and God Who sees in secret, will reward you." St. Therese not only hid her "fasting"; that is, her pain, suffering, and sacrifice from men, but also from herself and -- even, so to speak, from God Himself. She never complained, murmured, or felt sorry for herself in her heart. Nor did she complain or murmur in prayer. "God rejoices me by all that He does," repeated Therese in the silence of her heart.

Sick and dying people are usually unattractive, but such was not the case with St. Therese. Although she was dying and at times was in great pain, she maintained her cheerfulness and gave constant witness to the joy and peace of Christ. Her fellow nuns loved to visit her, and it was she who consoled, comforted, and refreshed their spirits. Therese died as she lived in the peace and joy of the Lord. A photograph taken just after her death shows a marvelous smile on her face.

We should try to imitate St. Therese, and reject from our hearts all negative thoughts, refrain from uttering a word of complaint, and remove from our attitude and demeanor any trace of sadness, irritation, or anger. By this practice of constant joy, we give glory to God, witness to Jesus, and pleasure to Mary, the smiling Virgin of the poor -- our mother, model, and mentor.

CHAPTER 15

THE VIRGIN OF THE POOR

Our Lady of Banneux is the patroness of the Sisters of Mary. She is also our model, mentor, and mother.

The apparitions at Banneux, Belgium, between January 15 and March 2 of 1933, are the last fully approved apparitions in the history of the Church. These apparitions have a beauty, dramatic conciseness, and depth of meaning very reminiscent of the joyful mysteries of the rosary. After reading of and reflecting upon the apparitions, one concludes that such beauty, clarity, simplicity, and depth could have originated only in Heaven.

The story of the apparitions is simple and briefly told.

The place is Banneux, Belgium -- a poor, insignificant hamlet in a small, insignificant country. Banneux, Belgium, at the time of the apparition resembled Nazareth of Palestine at the time of Jesus. As of Nazareth, it could be said of Banneux, "Can anything good possibly come from such a poor and lowly place?"

The time is January 15th, Sunday, 7:00 o'clock in the evening. The one chosen by Mary is Mariette Beco, age twelve -- the eldest child of a poor working man's family of seven children. Later on there would be four more additions to the Beco family.

In many respects, Mariette Beco at the time of the apparitions resembles Mary of Nazareth at the time of the annunciation. Frequently, when Mary chooses an individual for a special mission, she chooses one who resembles her and reflects her qualities, traits, and characteristics.

Mariette Beco is very young, as was Mary of Nazareth at the time of the annunciation. Mariette was blessed with a natural humility, simplicity, and lowliness -- all of which are Mary's outstanding characteristics. Although naturally humble, Mariette Beco possessed great strength of character, courage, and determination. Mary, the mother of Jesus, shows the same remarkable strength, courage, and determination throughout her entire life, but especially at the time of the passion and death of Jesus. Mary, courageously remained in the darkness of Calvary, spiritually nailed to the cross with Jesus until it was all over.

Like Mary, the ever virgin mother of God, so too Mariette Beco was most modest, pure, and chaste. Mariette Beco was candid, truthful, and frank -- almost to the point of being discourteous and offensive. Mary of Nazareth is also a virgin of light, and the mother of truth, who is her Son, Jesus. At the time of the first apparition Mariette Beco was looking after her baby brother who was ailing, and also at the same time anxiously waiting for her younger brother to return home, so that she could give him his supper. She was in the habit of self-sacrificing, helping, and serving others. Mary of Nazareth served her cousin, Elizabeth, for three months after the visitation, remaining with her to help out until the time of the birth of John the Baptist. Mary of Nazareth also showed her concern for others at the wedding feast of Cana, where she entrusts the need of the bride and groom into the hands of Jesus. In these and in many other little ways, Mariette Beco reminds us very much of Mary of Nazareth.

Mariette Beco is seated at the window of her small house looking out into the dark, winter night, watching and waiting for the return of her ten-year-old brother. Suddenly, the Virgin appears to her. She is clothed in white with a sky blue cincture tied about her waist. She is radiant, youthful, beautiful. In many respects, Mary resembles her son, Jesus, transfigured on Mount Thabor, where His face shone as the sun and His garments were white as snow.

This beautiful, radiant, young lady smiles at the child. She bends forward towards the child with her hands pointed downward in an attitude of motherly concern and personal respect. Tenderly, she motions to the child with her finger to come out to her.

The child is immediately captivated by this warm, tender, motherly love which Mary manifests throughout the apparitions. Mary is called the "mother of fair love." She is the mother of this new, "sweet" love which Jesus comes to teach. What is more, Mary does not hide this love in her heart; but she expresses it by the smile on her lips, the radiant expression on her face, the warm look in her eyes, her respectful gestures, her courteous words, her motherly actions. This is how she wins the heart of the child in order to lead her to Jesus.

In this first apparition the mother of God teaches us the meaning of the mission of the Sisters of Mary. We are called to win the hearts of the poor and the little ones by this new, sweet, smiling love of Jesus in order to lead them to the light of Jesus.

Mariette Beco takes out a rosary which she had found one day by the side of the road and begins reciting it. Then she excitedly calls to her mother that the Virgin is outside the window, asking her to come out. The mother rushes to the window, looks out, and, indeed, does see a strange light; but she interprets it as coming from a witch or a ghost. Then she quickly locks the door and forbids the child to go out. So ends the first apparition.

On Tuesday, Mariette Beco goes to Mass, and to the amazement of the parish priest, she attends catechism class. Not only that, but she has the answers to some of the catechetical questions which is something new and unusual for her. Her heart, already ensnared by this marvelous love of the Virgin, Mariette Beco wishes to respond by doing what she instinctively knows will please the "beautiful lady".

On Wednesday, January 18th, about seven in the evening, it is very cold, and pitch black outside. Although Mariette Beco has a great fear of the dark, she suddenly leaves the house, goes outside, kneels down on the cold, frozen earth, and then begins reciting the rosary. The Virgin appears to her again, her lips constantly moving in prayer. The Virgin gestures to the child, and then moves backwards, leading the child away from the house to a hidden stream down the road. The smiling Virgin has her arms extended, and leans toward the child -- very much resembling a mother teaching her child how to walk and ready to catch the child at the first sign of falling. Mary never turns her back on Mariette, once again showing the deepest respect for this poor, lowly, and underprivileged youngster. This scene reminds us of the words of Jesus in the Gospel, "Take care and do not despise even one of these little ones."

Mariette Beco responds gladly to the Virgin's gesture and begins following her. Suddenly, almost as if pushed by a hidden force, Mariette falls to the frozen earth. The thud of her knees striking the hard ground is distinctly heard by those witnessing the scene. This occurs twice. Then the Virgin points to a spring of water gushing from the frozen earth and says, "Plunge your hands into the water." Although the water is freezing cold, the child unhesitatingly does so. And in so doing she loses her rosary in the water. The Virgin speaks again, "This spring is reserved for me. Good night, au revoir." Then she disappears.

This spring of water is a symbol of the river of grace which flows from the wounded side of Jesus on the cross. Mary comes to lead the child to Jesus, in whom is the fullness of grace, life, and salvation. She leads the child by first capturing her heart with this new "sweet" love of Jesus, and then by getting the child to pray and sacrifice.

In all these apparitions, Mary speaks to the child, not as a queen to a subject, a master to a slave, or a teacher to a pupil; but rather as a loving mother to a daughter, or as a close friend to another. "Love is friendship," says St. Thomas Aquinas. Accordingly, Mary makes a friend of the child and always speaks to her, greets her, and treats her as an intimate friend. "Love," in the words of St. Paul, "is never discourteous." Accordingly, Mary the mother of God and the queen of Heaven always treats Mariette Beco with exquisite courtesy and respect.

Again about seven o'clock in the evening of Thursday, January 19th, the third apparition takes place. Mariette Beco sees the Virgin and exclaims, "Oh, here she is!" After a moment of silence the child asks, "Who are you, beautiful lady?" The "beautiful lady" replies, "I am the Virgin of the poor."

It is interesting to note that Mary does not identify herself as the "mother," the "helper," or the "refuge" of the poor, but rather as the "Virgin of the poor." By choosing this title, Mary indirectly reveals her great love of chastity and her special delight in purity. At the same time, she identifies herself with the poor, as did Jesus.

Jesus was anointed by the Spirit to announce the good news to the poor. He is known as "Jesus of Nazareth," which is to say "Jesus of the poor."

At the time of this third apparition Mariette Beco asks for a clarification of the previous apparition. She says, "Beautiful Lady, you said this spring was reserved for me. Why me?" Mariette Beco naively thinks the spring is reserved for herself, and this confuses her. The Virgin laughs gently and explains, "The spring is reserved for herself, the Virgin; for all nations, for the sick." Then the Virgin says, "I will pray for you. Goodbye."

Here Mary shows that she cannot only smile, but also laugh. Love, then is not only sweet and smiling, but it also has a delightful sense of humor.

Again, like Jesus, Mary also shows her great compassion for the sick and the suffering. She also reveals her universal outlook by stating the spring is not just for the sick of Banneux, or Belgium, or Europe -- but it is "for all nations."

In the same spirit, the Sisters of Mary are called upon to serve the poor and lowly not just of this or that country, but of all nations. They are to have the same breadth of vision and universal outlook as Jesus and Mary.

On Friday, January 20th, Mary appears for the fourth time. The child asks the question, "What do you want, beautiful lady?" The Virgin replies, "I would like a little chapel." Then, making the sign of the cross over the child, Mary disappears.

Mary, like Jesus, comes to serve; and again as Jesus, she comes to serve primarily in a spiritual manner. The greatest service is the saving of souls, and the greatest gift is the gift of faith, truth, and light. Accordingly, Mary does not say she wants an orphanage, a hospital, a school, or a library -- she wants a "little chapel". A chapel is a place of prayer, where the sacrifice of the Mass is offered, and where the Eucharist is honored and adored. In the Gospels it is recorded that Jesus comes primarily to save the people from sin, to deliver them from evil, to give them the fullness of life, and an abundance of grace. Mary indirectly reveals that she comes with the same intent and purpose.

From January 20th until Saturday, February 11th, Mariette Beco goes out every night waiting and watching for her friend and mother, the smiling "Virgin of the poor" to appear. But she waits and watches in vain. Her faith and trust are being put to the test, and indeed it is a cruel test for this innocent youngster.

Mariette Beco is mocked, taunted, and tormented by her schoolmates who get word of the apparitions. At school, the boys kneel mockingly before her and say, "Ooh, beautiful lady, give me your blessing." On at least one occasion the boys strike her, and Mariette returns home in the evening with her face black and blue. The girls greet her with a "Good morning, Bernadette." All this cuts the child to the quick, just as the heart of Mary was also pierced by a sword of humiliation. But Mariette remains faithful. Every night, whether it is raining or snowing, whether she is feeling well or not, she goes out, kneels on the cold earth, and recites one, two, sometimes as many as four, five, and six rosaries.

Mariette Beco passes this severe test and her humble patience is rewarded. On Saturday, February 11th, she is kneeling again outside the house, and after a few minutes she goes to the spring to kneel. The Virgin, then appears to her and says, "I come to relieve suffering. Goodbye."

These words of the Virgin once again echo the words of Christ in the Gospel. Christ says, "I have come to serve." Mary too comes to serve, to alleviate the sick, and to relieve the suffering -- especially of the poor, needy, and little ones.

On Wednesday, February 15th, at about the same time in the evening, the sixth apparition occurs. The child speaks, "Blessed Virgin, the parish priest has told me to ask you for a sign." The Virgin answers, "Believe in me, I will believe in you." Then she confides a secret to the child. When she is about to leave, the Virgin adds, "Pray very much. Goodbye."

"Believe in me, I will believe in you." These words are strikingly similar to those of Jesus in the Gospel of St. John where He says, "Abide in Me, I will abide in you." Just as Jesus begs for the faith and love of His friends, the apostles and disciples, Mary too with great respect asks for the belief and trust of this lowly child. Mary also proves that Mariette is indeed her special friend by entrusting to her a secret. Since only friends share secrets this is indeed a mark of special intimacy. In the Gospel Jesus tells His apostles, "I no longer call you servants but friends." And to prove that they are His friends, Jesus goes on to say, "I reveal to you all the secrets which the Father has revealed to Me."

On Monday, February 20th, the seventh apparition takes place. Mariette Beco kneels at the spring; and the Virgin, smiling as usual, tells her, "My dear child, pray very much." Then, with a serious expression and tone of voice, she bids her farewell with the words, "Goodbye, au revoir."

There is another "black-out" which lasts for many days. Mariette Beco goes out every night, and watches for the beautiful Lady to appear -- but again she waits and watches in vain. Finally, on Thursday, March 2nd, the Virgin appears again. Although it was raining heavily, the sky suddenly clears up, and the sparkling stars appear. So, too, does the Virgin. This time the Virgin looks serious. She does not smile, and with a grave tone of voice says, "I am the Mother of the Savior, Mother of God." Then, with a look of sadness on her face -- because this was to be her last visit with her close friend -- Mary gives Mariette her final word of advice, "Pray very much. Au revoir." She, then, lays her hands on the head of the child, blesses her with the sign of the cross, and leaves -- never to return again.

As Jesus in the Gospels embraces the children, and lays His hands on the head of the sick, Mary does the same with this child -- again manifesting her personal love and respect. There is a certain liturgy in this final apparition in which Mary entrusts the child with a mission. Mariette Beco is to give testimony to what she has seen and heard before the mighty and the learned of the Church with courage, clarity, and forcefulness.

Indeed after many years of intensive interrogation, exhaustive investigation, and painful examinations, the apparitions were declared fully authentic and worthy of belief. The Holy Father, Pope John Paul II, as a sign of formal approval of these apparitions, visited Banneux when he made his official visit to Belgium in the late 1980s.

"Like mother, like daughter." We are the daughters of Our Lady of Banneux, and as such we are called to be her witnesses. The "Virgin of the poor" is not well known. We are called to be a "living book" in which the faithful can easily read her message and learn her secrets. We must try to imitate the "Virgin of the poor" and model our lives after her. By resembling her in every way we show who she is, what she is like, and what are her goals and objectives.

We imitate the "Virgin of the poor" in our spirit of service of the poor, the lowly, the little ones, the sick, and the suffering. We try to serve them with this sweet, smiling, and tender love of Jesus and Mary. We try to win their hearts with this "new" love in order to lead them gently to Jesus. But this tender love is also a "tough" love. So we encourage those under our care to pray, to pray very much, to pray constantly. We also encourage them to sacrifice, to do penance, and to practice self-discipline.

As the "Virgin of the poor," we are called to pray constantly, and to pray especially for the poor entrusted to our care.

Finally, we are called to have a special faith in and love of the virtue of chastity, to practice it ourselves, and to try to inculcate it in the hearts, minds, and lives of all those entrusted to our care.

To remind ourselves of our vocation, and to be faithful to the "Virgin of the poor," we can recite frequently this simple Act of Consecration:

"O Mary, Our Lady of Banneux, Virgin of the poor, Mother of the Savior, Mother of God, I am totally yours.

I wish to be your child, your friend, your witness, your instrument, your servant, your slave.

O Mary, I wish you to be my mother, my friend, my protector, my helper, my guide, my queen.

O Mary, please lead me to Jesus in Whom is the fullness of grace, life, and love. Amen."

CHAPTER 16

THE CONSTITUTIONS AND VOWS

THE CONSTITUTIONS OF THE SISTERS OF MARY

CHARISM AND IDENTITY

1. A Sister of Mary shall pray three hours a day in imitation of Christ nailed to the cross.

   a) A Sister of Mary prays first for her own sanctification; and secondly, for the salvation of the poor -- entrusted to her care.

   b) The prayer of the Sisters of Mary is centered on the Eucharist (communion and adoration); on Mary (especially the rosary); and on the Saints (meditative reading of their lives and writings).

2. A Sister of Mary shall serve the poor -- especially needy children -- in the name of Christ.

   a) Service in the name of Christ is primarily: 1) self-sacrificing, 2) humble, and 3) spiritual.

   b) Service in the name of Christ is secondarily: kind, friendly, direct, personal, free, modern, complete, and universal.

PATRONESS

3. Our Lady of Banneux, "The Virgin of the poor," is the patroness of the Sisters of Mary.

This smiling Virgin of the poor, "who comes to relieve suffering," is the living book from whom the Sisters of Mary learn the nature of their calling and the essence of their charism.

MOTTO

4. The motto of the Sisters of Mary is: "Let us serve the Lord with joy!"

INVESTITURE

5. Shortly after her entry into the community -- at a time deemed appropriate by her Superior -- a candidate is given the habit of the Sisters of Mary to wear.

VOWS

6. After adequate formation -- including at least one year of novitiate -- the novice takes five vows of poverty, chastity, obedience, service of the poor, and three hours of daily prayer.
   a) The five vows are in honor of the five wounds of Christ.
   b) The vows are taken for a period of one year.
   c) The vows are renewed each year at the end of the annual retreat.

GOVERNMENT AND AUTHORITY

7. Upon the resignation or demise of the Founder, Sisters who have been in vows for at least ten years shall elect a Superior General by simple majority vote.
   a) The term of office of the Superior General is ten years.
   b) The Superior General can be re-elected indefinitely.
   c) The Superior General shall select two Assistants, who shall be called the First Assistant and the Second

Assistant. They shall constitute her
Advisory Council and assist in
administering the Society.

8. The Superior General shall exercise full
control of all fund raising organizations and
corporations of the Sisters of Mary.

9. No funds of the Sisters of Mary may be
allocated for projects or programs outside of
the direct control and responsibility of the
Sisters of Mary.

ADDENDA

1. When it is deemed useful for the good of the
poor whom the Sisters of Mary are called to
serve, they shall apply for formal recognition
and approval from the proper Church
authorities.

2. However, approval by God should be
considered more important than approval by
men; and recognition from heaven is more
desirable than recognition from earth. Christ
has said, "By their fruits, you shall know
them." By their fruits, the Sisters of Mary
can show that they have recognition and
approval from above. These fruits of charity
should be: 1) abundant in number,
2) excellent in quality, and 3) continuous in
duration. Such fruits are proof that the
Sisters of Mary are moved, guided, and
inspired by the Holy Spirit -- who above all is a
Spirit of love and Whose first charism is
charity.

FIRST VOWS

"O Mary, I am totally yours.

O Mary, conceived without sin, pray for me who have recourse to you.

O Mary, my Mother, I stand before you this morning, to make my first vows as a Sister of Mary of Banneux. At the same time, I wish to consecrate my life to you.

O Mary, at Banneux, you said: "I am the Virgin of the poor. I come to relieve suffering. Believe in me. I too will believe in you."

O Mary, I believe in you. And united with you, I believe in the poverty of Jesus. I believe that by renouncing all that I possess for Jesus, I will possess all things in Him. I believe that in the poverty of Jesus is found spiritual riches and eternal wealth.

O Mary, united with you, I believe in the chastity of Jesus. I believe that by renouncing all bodily pleasure for Jesus, I will possess all pleasure. I believe that by making this vow of chastity I become Jesus' special companion, friend, and spouse. I also believe that He will be with me all days even until the end of the world.

O Mary, united with you, I believe in the obedience of Jesus. I believe that in obedience is found the glorious freedom of the children of God and that peace of God which surpasses all understanding.

O Mary, I believe in a life of service. And united with you, I promise to serve the poor in the name of Jesus. I believe that to serve the poor is a honor, a grace, and a privilege. I believe that when I serve the poor, I serve Jesus -- and that whatsoever I do to one of His little ones, I do unto Him.

O Mary, I believe in the necessity of prayer. United with Jesus nailed to the cross, and with you standing at the foot of the cross, I promise to pray three hours each day.

With these beliefs firmly rooted in my heart, I Sister _____ do hereby vow for a period of one year poverty, chastity, obedience, service of the poor, and prayer in accordance with the spirit, the rules, and the constitutions of the Sisters of Mary of Banneux.

At the same time, I wish to consecrate my life and vocation to Mary, our Lady of Banneux, Virgin of the poor, and my Mother.

O Mary, I am totally yours.

O Mary, conceived without sin, pray for me who have recourse to you."

(Signed)

(Date)

RENEWAL OF VOWS

"O Mary, I am totally yours.

O Mary, conceived without sin, pray for me who have recourse to you.

O Mary, my Mother, I stand before you this morning, to renew my vows as a Sister of Mary of Banneux. At the same time, I wish to renew the consecration of my life to you.

O Mary, at Banneux, you said: "I am the Virgin of the poor. I come to relieve suffering. Believe in me. I too will believe in you."

O Mary, I believe in you. And united with you, I believe in the poverty of Jesus. I believe that by renouncing all that I possess for Jesus, I will possess all things in Him. I believe that in the poverty of Jesus is found spiritual riches and eternal wealth.

O Mary, united with you, I believe in the chastity of Jesus. I believe that by renouncing all bodily pleasure for Jesus, I will possess all pleasure. I believe that by making this vow of chastity I become Jesus' special companion, friend, and spouse. I also believe that He will be with me all days even until the end of the world.

O Mary, united with you, I believe in the obedience of Jesus. I believe that in obedience is found the glorious freedom of the children of God and that peace of God which surpasses all understanding.

O Mary, I believe in a life of service. And united with you, I promise to serve the poor in the name of Jesus. I believe that to serve the poor is an honor, a grace, and a privilege. I believe that when I serve the poor, I serve Jesus -- and that whatsoever I do to one of His little ones, I do unto Him.

O Mary, I believe in the necessity of prayer. United with Jesus, nailed to the cross and with you standing at the foot of the cross, I promise to pray three hours each day.

With these beliefs firmly rooted in my heart, I Sister _____ do hereby renew for a period of one year the vows of poverty, chastity, obedience, service of the poor, and prayer in accordance with the spirit, the rules, and the constitutions of the Sisters of Mary of Banneux.

At the same time, I wish to renew the consecration of my life and vocation to Mary, Our Lady of Banneux, Virgin of the poor and my Mother.

O Mary, I am totally yours.

O Mary, conceived without sin, pray for me who have recourse to you."

(Signed)

(Date)